Buildings Nature Cities

Buildings Nature Cities

Andrew Bromberg at Aedas

Introduction and Essays by Aaron Betsky

300+ illustrations

Thames & Hudson

On the cover: Sandcrawler (front; see also pages 142–43), photograph by
Paul Warchol; Nanfung Commercial, Hospitality and Exhibition Complex
(back; see also page 86), photograph by Marcus Oleniuk.

Page 2: Sandcrawler, photograph by Paul Warchol.

Buildings, Nature, Cities: Andrew Bromberg at Aedas © 2018
Thames & Hudson Ltd, London

Text © 2018 Andrew Bromberg at Aedas
Introduction and essays © 2018 Aaron Betsky

Sketches, drawings and plans © 2018 Andrew Bromberg at Aedas
For all other illustrations, please see the picture credits list at
the end of the book

Designed by Praline

First published in 2018 in the United States of America
by Thames & Hudson Inc., 500 Fifth Avenue, New York,
New York 10110

www.thamesandhudsonusa.com

Library of Congress Control Number 2017959864

ISBN 978-0-500-51965-3

Printed in China by Shanghai Offset Printing Products Limited

CONTENTS

The Third Landscape
Aaron Betsky

This book is the result of five walks that I took with the Hong Kong-based architect Andrew Bromberg during the summer of 2016. When I first made Bromberg's acquaintance, he took me on one of his regular hikes up to the Peak, the steep mountain that dominates yet in some ways merges with the skyscrapers, apartment blocks and shopping malls that define the human-made geology of the island. He takes these walks several times a week as a kind of 'walking meditation'. His love for both what we as humans have made and for the forms of nature we encountered was evident as we made our way up to the top of the island and surveyed its forms in all their jostling and expressive juxtaposition. As we were walking, we spoke of the seminal project the late Zaha Hadid had designed in 1982 for the Peak's summit. It was a proposed residential club she showed as the result of the mountain and the buildings on the slopes shedding planes that then recombined to form the club's gyrating walls, ceilings and floors. As we talked, I also recalled the drawings Bromberg had made during his travels around Asia, which evidenced his deep understanding of place as both humans and nature had shaped its forms.

We then decided to make a book that would explore how this architect's work, which is located mostly in Asia and the Middle East, although he is also working in Europe and North America, comes out of, interprets, condenses and opens up the landscapes in which he works. Our theory was that at the core of his work is an attempt to understand the nature of and differences between the forms, images, textures and spaces humans produce, and what nature has given us. Rather than replacing the existing world with an artificial one, Bromberg tries to weave these together and find a way in which a third, hybrid reality can emerge.

To figure out how this might work, we agreed to visit as many of Bromberg's built works as we could, and also to make a trip together to the Rocky Mountains outside of Denver, where Bromberg grew up. The record of those walks provided the material out of which the texts in this book emerged. We walked through Hong Kong, Singapore, Dubai and Guangzhou, in areas where Bromberg had designed or built structures. The aim was not so much to view those buildings in themselves, but to try to understand how they came out of, responded to, and perhaps offered alternatives to those neighbourhoods. We also walked through significant areas in these cities, such as the Peak, the Creek area of Dubai, and the forest park at the centre of Singapore, as a way to understand their history, climate and geology. We drove through these cities together, and we visited Bromberg's office, speaking with his associates and clients to come to a fuller understanding of how he worked.

In walking and talking, Bromberg and I soon came to realize that finding specific elements or forms of influence that were either human-made or natural was not as easy as we had assumed, while identifying the specifics of each landscape in which a building he had designed appeared also proved complicated. That is because he works — like many successful architects — in a third landscape: one defined by international flows of capital, images and ideas. It is also a context that bears the distinct marks of building production methods, regulations and use patterns (an office building or an apartment building is more or less the same everywhere in terms of its functions, but so are theatres and shopping malls). This third landscape by its very nature combines specific sites with abstract forms, but also shapes buildings according to contours that seem to come out of nowhere, or at least whose driving forces are invisible to the untrained eye. How a building appears might have as much to do with the price and availability of glass or steel, or with the logic of elevators, as it does with either soil conditions and wind patterns, for example, or the surrounding buildings and public spaces.

Moreover, Bromberg — again, like most architects — has developed a predilection for certain forms and images that he refines and develops over time. The slow curves of his towers contrast with his interest in stacking forms for lower buildings into tubes or rectangular volumes, while his public spaces often appear in wedge-shaped or billowing cladding that makes their importance and their function as places that are full of human energy clear. He has his own signature, and a style that is all his own.

You might make much the same arguments for the environments in which most of us live. They are shaped by where they are, and

how they grew in that place. They have what critics call
a vernacular. Rain, heat, the steepness and direction of slopes,
the flows of water, views, the nature of the soil and the
vegetation of a place are still present and still form the places
where we work, live and play. However, they do so in relation
to what we have made out of those places over time, which is
to say, the historical happenstance of how buildings and streets
appear. Thus a place might also be shaped by which particular
colonial power – with all its prejudices and tastes – was present
at a given time. It will also appear in such a manner as a result
of the increasingly homogeneous codes, regulations, financial
desires, tastes and use patterns that define our daily lives –
a kind of international vernacular. Within these places and all
the force fields, visible and invisible, which are present there,
architects then try to make structures that have an identity
and character that makes them particular – and beautiful.

Bromberg has achieved this in many of his buildings, despite
the vagaries of current building practices, and especially
the many constraints on the making of good designs that confront
architects today. Throughout this process, Andrew Bromberg
has become an architect who drinks in, reinterprets, and remakes
the complicated context that is our current reality. He has
succeeded better than most, and has indeed produced beautiful
places in which to work, play and live.

HONG KONG: CLIMBING THE PEAK

Varanasi, India (1995), by Andrew Bromberg. Density: labyrinth
of streets; daylight on the banks of the Ganges, bustling with life
(and death) rituals.

Two or three times a week, Denver-born architect Andrew Bromberg leaves his apartment in Hong Kong's Tin Hau and sets out across Victoria Park, which he looks over from his twelfth-floor window. He passes through the shopping streets that weave their way along this mountain city's lower flanks, then ascends the Peak, the 550 m (1,804 ft) high ridge that rises steeply in the centre of the island. He does not stop for coffee, to shop or to see any sights. He climbs quickly, reaching the visitor centre and shopping mall at the Peak's highest point in a little over an hour.

Bromberg has no particular reason to speed-walk like this so often. Once at the top he sometimes has lunch, but often just continues downhill, passing his favourite rubber tree that has grown around boulders and a stone. Park authorities prevented it from tumbling down the hill by pouring concrete to one side, making it somewhere between a natural and a human-made object, of which Bromberg says: 'This rock sums up Hong Kong for me… it just feels like this is what you do here. You admire and cherish nature, but then you flow all around it, cover it up, turn into something that is new.'

'This sums up Hong Kong for me; it just feels like this is what you do here. You admire and cherish nature, but then you flow all around it, cover it up, turn it into something new'

His route then takes him past the base of some of the hybrid hotels, shopping malls and office buildings that translate the Peak's mass into its human equivalent. He finds his way back to Tin Hau before leaving for his office at Hong Kong's eastern edge, in an area called Quarry Bay. There he runs his own studio at Aedas, a 1,200-person design firm with offices around the world.

'I do it because it keeps me alive and thinking,' Bromberg says of his morning walk. 'It is a form of walking meditation. I don't see things directly, but I notice them and I keep myself

moving. I recalibrate myself to Hong Kong.' Like many successful
architects, he is usually in motion at a much faster pace,
working on commissions around the world. The morning I joined
him on his walk he had just arrived from Dubai, where a new
hotel will join several office buildings and apartment towers
to his designs that are already built, and Singapore, where
he has designed
a 5,000-seat theatre
and a campus for
Lucasfilm, George
Lucas's animation
division, and
is now designing
a new headquarters
for the local
transport authority.
He was scheduled
to go to Beijing
the following day
for another project.
It is one
of the ironies
of the modern world
that architecture,
which is about

Florence, Italy (1993), by Andrew Bromberg. Density: the two
sides of the city are joined together by the markets of the
Ponte Vecchio.

making things that are rooted to the ground and that shelter
us in place, is created by designers who often spend more time
in aeroplanes and hotels than they do in their homes. This is
certainly true when they start designing large office buildings,
apartment blocks and large-scale cultural, transportation
or recreational structures. Such architecture not only has
a scale that demands international investment, but also consists
on the whole of materials that are mass produced elsewhere,
and assembled on site. The rules and regulations that govern
architecture are almost always the same everywhere, and the
buildings that arise are the results as much of global flows
of capital as they are of local needs.
    Despite his travels, and steeled by his walks, Bromberg
holds on to the conviction that architecture should be about the
translation of a site into form, which he then sculpts using his
interpretations of both local culture and the logic of a global

economy. Of course, his work is still subject to the restrictions of standardized materials, functions and regulations. While he is travelling, he sketches and looks hard at the landscape, both natural and human-made, to understand how he should design in all the places he works.

Bromberg is interested in how the natural environment shapes its human equivalent - and not just at the scale of building materials, or when considering the size of windows to admit sunlight, or how steep the roofs need to be to protect a building from rain or snow. He is also interested in how our collective structures, our cities and our suburbs, result from geology, climate and ecosystems; their relation to a larger landscape of oceans and continents; and how the places we make then reshape and deform the landscapes from which they came.

It is his way of building his own bit of Hong Kong. As somebody who grew up at the foot of the Rocky Mountains, Bromberg feels at home in the presence of a nature that is much larger than anything humans have made and that always looks over us. In Hong Kong, while human beings have made a great effort to equal the geology they found, they have also respected nature. For decades, the British severely restricted building across the colony. In one sense, they were continuing the Asian tradition that you live only in the valleys, leaving the mountains to contain and frame the scene, while building mainly religious structures and retreats on their flanks. To the British, it was also a question of security, as they sought to stay away from their threatening neighbour to the north. To real-estate developers, the system was a boon: they became wealthy by developing what they could with an intensity that became famous around the world, producing dense packs of towers that are where all but the very rich and a few holdouts in the backcountry live.

It is that combination of geology and planning that has given Hong Kong its modern character. The most notable feature of Hong Kong was its deep harbour, protected by the island while permitting direct access to the hinterland. That sheltered place for ships is, in turn, connected to the Pearl River Delta, which lets boats travel up to Guangzhou and beyond, while also giving access to the rich agricultural fan spreading south. The city developed on the island rather than the facing shore of Kowloon for that protection and isolation, and because the most common way to transport people or goods was by water.

The culture of sampans, the basic units of transportation and fishing that were also home to their owners, created a new surface on top of the harbour: a sea of boats tethered together, lapping at the shores and detaching to go out on their journeys.

Bologna, Italy (1993), by Andrew Bromberg. Density: Dante's leaning towers provide a frame of reference for the surrounding Gothic urban fabric.

Above these two layers the city rose in rows, stepping up the gentle slopes to the south. The wealthiest moved ever further away from the noise, smells and danger of the harbour, occupying ground steadily closer to the sharp ridges of the Peak. Over the years, their homes crept all the way to the top, so that rows of houses and apartment buildings now cover the mountain's northern side, interrupted only by gardens, religious preserves and former military camps that have now become public parks. The city produced its own layer over the mountain, with stucco, concrete and glass replacing the vegetation, both native and imported, that turned the Peak into a carpet woven in green.

Then Hong Kong shot up, especially after the Second World War, producing what at one point was the densest agglomeration of towers in the world. Because space was so limited, and the influx of refugees, first from the Japanese and the Chinese Civil War, and then from the Communist regime, was so large, there was no place to go but up. A lack of zoning regulations permitted the construction of slender towers quite close to each other, while the immigrants, used to living and working in cramped quarters, were willing to accept very small spaces that could fit on narrow plots extruded up into the sky.

Over the years, the dense neighbourhoods of Wan Chai, Sheung Wan, Mid-Levels and Sai Wan became residential areas, rising over

what were originally workshops, while the downtown area grew up
into office blocks more like those to be found in other urban
cores around the world. As in most Asian cities, narrow streets
lined with stores filled in the bases and the leftover spaces
between these towers.

What made Hong Kong different was not only the layering
of these streets as long strands running one slightly above
the other along the slope in the east-west direction, but also
the network that wove all of this together. 'It's these networks
that bring people down from the towers, but also across the
streets, to the ferries, and up the mountain that make Hong
Kong's character,' Bromberg notes. You can now walk all
the way from one of the ferries, or from the train station

As in most Asian cities, narrow streets lined with stores filled in the bases and the leftover spaces between towers

that brings you in from
the airport, across the
rows of streets, through
shopping mall after
shopping mall, directly
on to an escalator that
takes you halfway up
the Peak, or to the tram
that takes you up to the
top. Though the system
started as a means
to bring passengers
arriving on the ferries
across the final strand
of the parallel streets, a bundle of major thoroughfares that
hugs the island's northern coast with an unending stream
of traffic, the resulting web of diagonal walkways moving in
and out of buildings has since spread across the territory.

Modern architects have long proposed 'streets in the air'
to enable residents to reach shops and community spaces without
interference from traffic, while delivery, parking and storage
would all be below them. In practice, these devices never seem
to be very attractive - possibly because they have been tried
in low-income housing developments, where they did not have
proper maintenance support - but here the raised pedestrian
zone worked beautifully.

The logic of these hybrids between pedestrian streets
and shopping arcades derives not so much from the ways in which

people have traditionally transformed natural landscapes into a network of human connectors, as it does from the enclosed shopping mall developed in the United States in the 1950s (the first of these, the Southdale Center, opened outside Minneapolis in 1956). Their success depends on removing you as much as possible from any direct connection to the outside world, other than through skylights. Not only are they generally windowless, but their design depends on diagonals and other geometric devices that skew you away from either the urban grid or surrounding natural landmarks. There is a method to this disorientation: it is meant to induce the so-called Gruen transfer, named after the architect who invented the concept. This is the moment

Hong Kong's innovation was to layer this mixed-use network on top of the streets rather than bury it underground

when the directed shopper, who came in with a particular purpose such as buying a shirt or a pair of shoes, is distracted by something else and starts wandering. There is a good chance this customer will then purchase things they had not intended to buy. And once it has you there, the mall also tries to keep you there with 'sticky' attractions that might have started out as a few places where kids could play or adults have a cup of coffee, but that have by now grown to a scale where some malls are fully fledged entertainment districts or even amusement parks as well as consumer labyrinths.

In Asia, the logic of such malls first combined with transportation systems in the central urban train stations of Japanese cities such as Tokyo and Osaka in the 1970s. The underground corridors were a means to tie together the long-distance, suburban and intra-urban train systems that, because of these cities' size and density, meant stations could easily take up the equivalent area of six square blocks. All along the connectors stores opened up, starting as informal stalls and over the years turning into legitimate businesses. Developers tied to the suburban train companies eventually took over,

turning these combinations of infrastructure and consumer havens
into layers of shopping malls, hotels and office buildings
in districts such as Shinjuku, Shibuya and downtown Tokyo.

Hong Kong's innovation was to layer this mixed-use network
on top of the streets rather than bury it underground. In the
original complexes, which fan out from the ferry piers, such
malls' development is visible in space as well as time. The ones
closest to the water are the most informal, eventually turning
into proto-malls with small shops crammed together without any
relief or place to gather. As you move up and out, crossing more
of the parallel roads, the malls become newer, larger and more
upscale, eventually turning into the kind of temples to luxury
surmounted by hotels and office buildings you can now find
anywhere in the world.

What sets all the Hong Kong webs apart is that they have
a rhythm of open and closed space. You move in and out of
buildings, and every time you cross a road you become aware,
if only for a moment, of where you are. The mall might isolate
you, but as you move along your commute, or from one shopping
opportunity to another, you are always aware of your place in the larger landscape. In the central district, you also keep losing your sense of elevation as the ground slopes up underneath you, so that you enter on a second or even third or fourth floor, then find yourself exiting directly on to the street at the rear.

Siena, Italy (1993), by Andrew Bromberg. Density: the sloping
roofs describe the patterns of the streets below.

If you keep going south in most of these malls on Hong
Kong Island, you eventually confront a slope so severe that
it constrains the mall's spread. At one point you can move -
via a lift, or stairs and escalators - on to the tiered campus
of Hong Kong University, which transforms the same mechanisms

into an academic precinct where classrooms, offices and cafeterias replace the shops and restaurants. At another point, you can transfer on to escalators that ride the Peak's ridge for several blocks, giving residents at higher elevations easy access to their apartments.

'No place has a more perfect layering of what we have made over the landscape than Hong Kong,' Bromberg says of the system, even though he avoids it most of the time by walking on the street or taking taxis. 'The malls are like grottos, the shopping streets like paths you take along the mountain.' What is remarkable is that the system is replicated all across the territory, even when there is no significant terrain change to justify the levels. There are connected malls in Kowloon, but even farther afield, in the forests of high-rise apartments that have grown up along stops on the commuter rail lines, this same system of raised streets and public spaces spreads out towards the edges of the residential areas, encompassing the towers themselves and becoming a connected communal base for a human-made 'peak' of concrete skyscrapers.

Rome, Italy (2000), by Andrew Bromberg. Density: the scale of the Baths of Caracalla punctuates the size of ancient Rome.

The buildings higher up do not fall away or turn into single-family homes and other small structures, as you would expect in other cities built on the slopes of mountains. Instead, the apartment buildings just become a bit looser in their arrangement, but also bulkier as they assimilate the parking on the slope. You feel as if you are rising up through canyons made by humans to extend the slope. Then you enter a park, and the density of these structures gives way to the jungle vegetation that still remains in the protected parts of what is officially Victoria Peak Park. You might think yourself in a version of what the island was before humans arrived and, in terms of the sheer bulk of vegetation, you could be, but a good portion of those plants are not native, having arrived either in an attempt to create cash crops or as stowaways among the goods the Westerners brought with them.

Bromberg says of Hong Kong: 'I see Hong Kong as the Asian equivalent of the type of city I've always resonated with. Mountains and sea, park and dense city. That is it for me. 'He elaborates: 'One of my favourite places in all of China is a bamboo park in Chengdu. It is mammoth bamboo, 20 or 30 m (65-100 ft) tall. While hiking on the western slope of the Peak in Hong Kong, all the trees lean in one direction, filtering the light. Here there's no consistent direction of wind, but the trees all have a lean towards the west. For me, it is all about leaning towards the light. I like to think everything moves towards the light.'

Hong Kong's human peaks have been layered in time, like the geological strata of the Peak itself. Near the harbour were the older structures, although some of them were replaced by new tower blocks thrusting up, doing the work that earthquakes managed for mountains as they turned lower valleys into new pinnacles, with structures whose smooth skins of glass and polished metal are as unweathered as stone freshly risen from the earth. Above some remaining flats that traced the plains were the higher structures, forming ridges that ran at angles to the Peak as they followed the streets moving upward. Then came the newer buildings, apartment blocks replacing the few private mansions that still clung to the Peak's higher elevations, until they too stopped only slightly below the ridge. The parks formed green valleys between these ridges, but they were not quite continuous, as streets and their buildings interrupted their flow. Only there did nature reassert itself, complete with waterfalls and rocks sticking up through the vegetation, but you never had a sense of its purity. In Hong Kong, it is hard to discern the difference between what was there and what we have made, to experience the two separately, or to take in the relationship between these layers of real and quasi-real geology.

Slightly below the ridge are the best views over the whole territory. Surrounded by parks, you can appreciate the ridges and planes, the whole of Hong Kong jamming together into a kaleidoscope of geometries. It all makes sense from there: the structures form a new landscape, one inhabited and used at every level, constantly eroding and thrusting back up ever higher than the one before.

Near the top of the Peak, Bromberg can pause on his hike and look out over his own, condensed version of this landscape. The new station for the high-speed train that connects Hong Kong to Shenzhen and Guangzhou is in some ways a continuation of Bromberg's trek to the Peak: an ascent from a high-speed train station deep underground, up through a corkscrewing space towards an artificial mountain. It is the architect's first design to be constructed in his adopted hometown. He won the commission to design the station in a competition in 2009. 'What you see is just a small part of the whole project,' he explains. 'It is the face of one of the world's longest tunnels, which runs all the way to Shenzhen. You will go down after you leave the station on the mainland and not emerge again until you come out here.'

The train station sprawls over a vast area of artificial land created a few years earlier, by digging into what had been water not too long before. Bromberg says of the station: 'there are nine platforms for short-haul trains, and then nine platforms for high-speed trains. Above that are all the customs and ticket sales and, of course, the retail. Then there is the big arch to contain it all, but, just as important, this artificial landscape above it. It is one of the few places in Hong Kong where the Lion's Peak in the distance is visible, and we want to preserve that view. There are height restrictions. The competition was based on the station, and how it functioned. From that, we proposed the civic use on top, turning the roof into a public park space. After winning the competition it was a lot of work to get the below-ground spaces figured out. The accessible roof was one piece the client never messed with. The value of that civic gesture was important to them.' The sheer scale of the work is staggering; the construction site as beautiful in its way as a finished building. Bromberg explains that this is why his aim in the completed station is 'to keep as much of the excitement of the structure visible and bathed in light'.

From the Peak, the station looks like a metal dragon rising out of the ground, its site sprawling over acres of land and part of a redevelopment of the whole northeast side of Kowloon. What was once one of the world's busiest harbour fronts will soon be the site of millions of square feet of office and housing, anchored by a new cultural centre. The train station is the first part of Hong Kong's newest version of itself to approach completion.

Hong Kong is already the site of massive infrastructure projects that have changed both the former colony's actual landscape and our perceptions of it. You once arrived in the harbour to the island's north, sailing between islands scattered across the South China Sea, and arriving with the Peak looming over you on one side and the ranges reaching back to the mainland receding on the Kowloon side.

'My aim is to keep as much of the excitement of the structure visible and bathed in light'

Even when aeroplanes replaced boats as the main mode of arrival, the airport was right on the harbour, and the final approach was famous (and famously dangerous), surrounded by apartment blocks.

The route from Shenzhen on the mainland was even more of a staged introduction, moving from village to village between the mountains and their covering of semi-tropical trees and plants. Closer to Kowloon, the density and the scale of the settlements gradually increased, with the massed apartment towers echoing the hills all around them and forming built canyons. When you finally arrived on Kowloon's plateau, you wound your way between these towering human habitations, arriving in the train station at the far end, where the city of Hong Kong revealed itself across the water, its line of skyscrapers stretching out below the Peak.

When the airport moved to Chek Lap Kok, an artificial island off the west coast of Hong Kong's sister island, Lantau, you lost that sense of the island rising out of the sea. Planes generally

Jaisalmer, India (1994), by Andrew Bromberg. Density: utility poles
interlaced within the deserted historic city streets.

approach from the water, and you now arrive in the middle of Norman Foster's undulating terminal before taking a train or taxi downtown. Along the way, you see clusters of high-rises along the waterside. As you get closer, they press around you, but as you soar over bridges and career through tunnels, you get little sense of being part of the landscape. A quick glance at the new container harbour, which moved around the same time as the airport away from the space between Kowloon and Hong Kong Island, and you are in the city itself, arriving in a maze of transport hub and shopping mall.

The new bullet train will compress the sequence further, which is why Bromberg considered the staged revelation of the city so important. The train will speed along in the dark all the way from Shenzhen, then come to a sudden halt. Bromberg's original intention was to reveal the sky as soon as the train stopped, but the need for fire compartmentation did not allow for porosity in the floor right above the train. Now you will move up towards and through customs, and begin to see the light through a large 45-m (148-ft) high volume, connecting five levels above. 'I wanted to draw you up, make you want to go to the city,' the architect explains.

As is the case in train stations around the world, the facility will also be a large shopping mall and real-estate development – and in this way also a reflection of Hong Kong itself. The twisting interior shopping streets will wind their way through and up the building mass, leading you to the transit connections that can take you further. Above you, towers will rise up into the sky above a jagged park that covers the massive steel trusses that are necessary to make the structure work.

As you make your way via the transport links and the shopping and eating places that are an intrinsic part of all modern transport hubs, you will keep turning, guided around and up by trusses and walls. These structures are Bromberg's signature: a calligraphy in glass and steel that curves and warps his buildings out of the straight and narrow. The building is a distillation not only of the city in which it sits, but also of Bromberg's design methodology.

Most people will see little of Kowloon, let alone the city across the bay, before they scurry off into subways, taxis or buses. But if you are waiting for somebody, or have some time to spare, it will be worth following the building's curves up all

the way to where they cross the main departure hall. It is
not just a roof: it is a new piece of landscape you can ascend
on ramps, moving past layers of landscape until you arrive
25 m (80 ft) above the ground, from where you can finally see
Hong Kong proper. 'I imagine people coming here to admire the
view, or to watch the fireworks,' Bromberg says. 'It actually
will be one of the largest parks in Hong Kong.'

After surveying the station and the new landscape he has
created, Bromberg can re-enter the one he inhabits. Moving down
the path and into the parks and the shadow of the high-rises
that jut up from the streets below, the station disappears,
and there is welcome shade. Traffic intensifies, and you are
engulfed in the Hong Kong that is without beginning or end,
just a jumble of activity and its frozen sediment in roads,
bridges and buildings. You are no longer tracing the landscape,
but part once again of its enveloping reality.

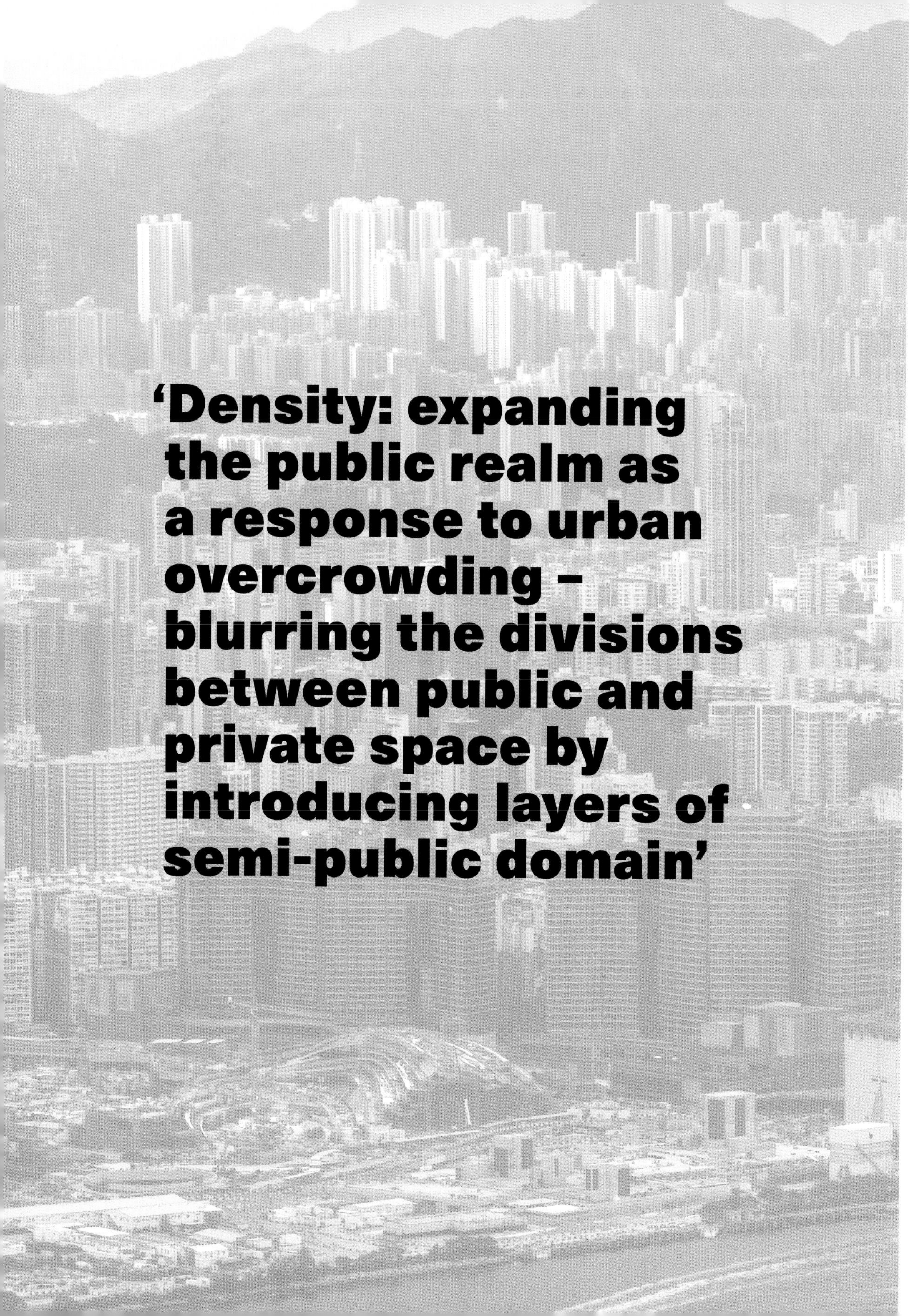

'Density: expanding
the public realm as
a response to urban
overcrowding –
blurring the divisions
between public and
private space by
introducing layers of
semi-public domain'

West Kowloon Station

Hong Kong SAR, China
Status: Built (2018)
GFA: 430,000 m² (4,628,481 ft²)
Site Area: 58,797 m² (632,886 ft²)
Building Height: 29 m (95 ft)

This underground high-speed rail terminus will connect Hong Kong to Beijing via the largest rail network in history. Located centrally in Hong Kong, within the city's existing urban realm, the 430,000 m² (4.6 million ft²) facility with fifteen tracks will be the largest below-ground station terminus in the world. The site's prominence immediately adjacent to the future West Kowloon Cultural District and next to Victoria Harbour required a design that was completely motivated by civic demand.

Within the station itself, there was one underlying goal of the scheme. Acting as the 'gateway' to Hong Kong, it was considered vital to connect the station with the surrounding urban context and make the traveller aware of their arrival or departure, announcing: 'You are in Hong Kong.' To achieve this, the design compacted all of the supporting spaces more efficiently to allow for a very large void down into the departure hall below. The outside ground plane bends down towards the hall, and the roof structure above gestures towards the harbour. The result is a 45-m (148-ft) high volume which focuses all attention through the south façade towards views of the Hong Kong Central skyline and Victoria Peak beyond.

The organization of the design was inspired by the idea of forces converging on Hong Kong – likened to the converging tracks coming into the station. The project maximizes civic gestures both internally and externally. What is highly unusual here is that the station will have an immigration domain for both Hong Kong and China in the same facility, as opposed to the way immigration works in a typical international airport, which is solely the domain of the host country.

The pedestrian paths flow up and access almost the entire rooftop of the station itself, 25 m (82 ft) above ground, in a densely vegetated sculpture garden and landscaped extension of the green below. The resulting 3.5-hectare (8.5-acre) open space offers a spectacular public vista over Victoria Harbour and towards Hong Kong's skyline.

Entrance building exterior, looking south

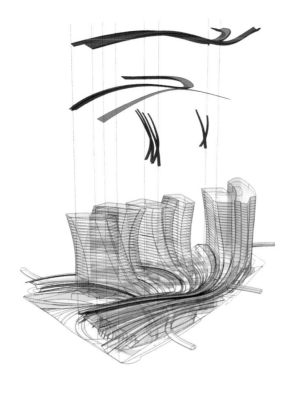

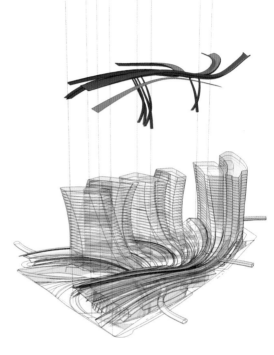

Entrance building diagrams, structural concept
for roof

Entrance building interior, north columns
of the 'big void' during construction

West elevation and civic square, looking south

Aerial view, looking east

'Double X column', looking south, within the
'big void'

Looking north into the 'big void'

Cross-section through the station

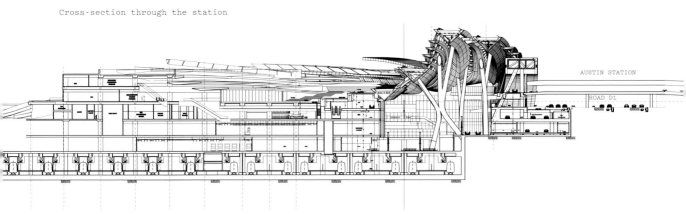

AUSTIN STATION

ROAD D1

'Double X column', structural diagrams

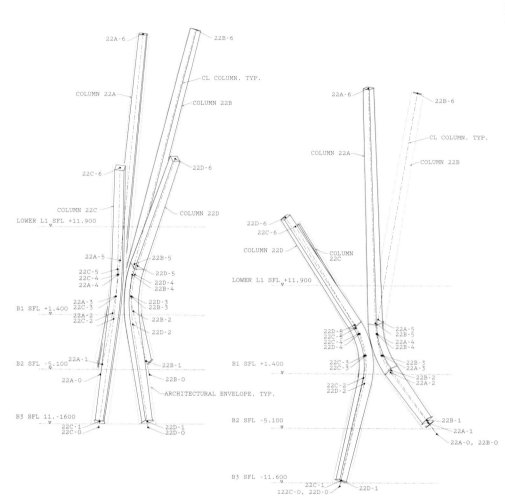

22A-6
22B-6
CL COLUMN. TYP.
COLUMN 22A
COLUMN 22B
22C-6
22D-6
COLUMN 22C
COLUMN 22D
LOWER L1 SFL +11.900
22A-5   22B-5
22C-5   22D-5
22C-4   22D-4
22A-4   22B-4
22A-3   22D-3
22C-3   22B-3
22A-2   22B-2
22C-2
B1 SFL +1.400   22D-2
22A-1   22B-1
22A-0   22B-0
ARCHITECTURAL ENVELOPE. TYP.
B3 SFL 11.-1600
22C-1   22D-1
22C-0   22D-0

22A-6
22B-6
CL COLUMN. TYP.
COLUMN 22A
COLUMN 22B
22D-6
22C-6
COLUMN 22D   COLUMN 22C
LOWER L1 SFL +11.900
22D-5   22A-5
22C-5   22B-5
22C-4   22A-4
22D-4   22B-4
22C-3   22B-3
B1 SFL +1.400   22A-3
22C-2   22B-2
22D-2   22A-2
B2 SFL -5.100   22B-1
22A-1
22A-0, 22B-0
B3 SFL -11.600
22C-1   22D-1
122C-0, 22D-0

Longitudinal section through the station

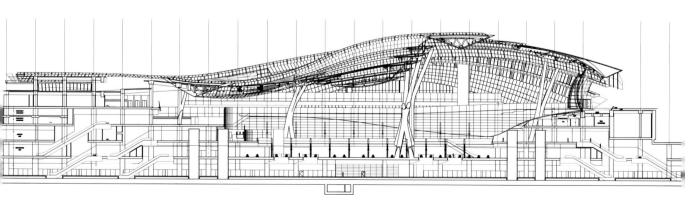

Entrance building, west and south elevations

Rendering, west elevation and
civic square

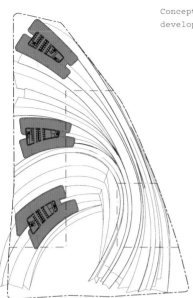

Conceptual diagram linking the future top-side development with the entrance building

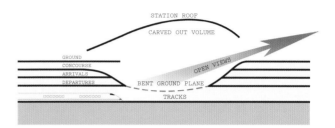

Diagram from the competition, describing the intent of the 'big void'

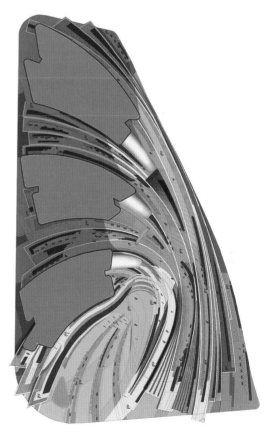

Landscape diagram of the station and its integration with the future top-side development

South elevation

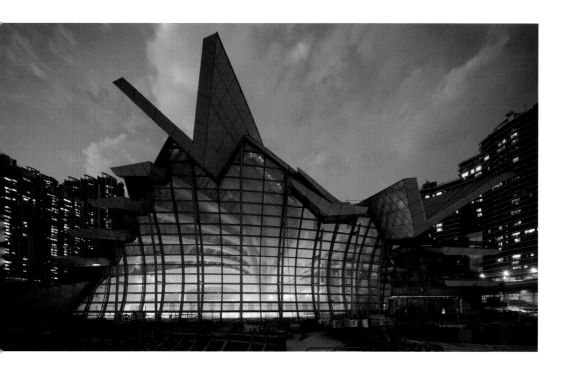

East elevation and eastern arch

Departure hall, looking south

'Double X column' in the eastern hall,
looking south

Alam Sutera Residence

Jakarta, Indonesia
Status: Construction (2020)
GFA: 56,471 m² (607,849 ft²)
Site Area: 8,000 m² (86,111 ft²)
Building Height: 135 m (443 ft)

Located in Serpong, Tangerang Regency, about 13 km west of the Jakarta CBD, the Alam Sutera Residence will be the focal point of Alam Sutera district. Despite the project's density and iconic scale it softly integrates itself within the site with its abundant green spaces throughout the complex. These garden spaces create communal sanctuaries for the residents while reflecting the surrounding tropical Jakartan landscapes.

The project is comprised of two towers linked intermittently with bridges. The towers are situated to maximize views out towards the CBD while carefully orienting for optimal day lighting. Balconies texture the elevations giving the users a chance to reconnect with the outdoors while also allowing natural shading for the units below. Open-air corridors within cores induce airflow currents for natural cooling and comfort.

The towers share a podium containing a clubhouse with a 30-m (100-ft) long infinity-edge swimming pool, sports courts and fitness facilities. The mid levels are inter-connected with a sky bridge linking a central garden space to encourage communal interaction.

The vertical expression of the project focuses importance on the roofscape. Lush multi-terraced gardens in the sky and a 50-m (160-ft) long sky pool are linked together 142 m (470 ft) above for tenants' accessibility. The exclusive gardens and pool elevate above and away from the city for a unique experience. Users re-engage the city from a new perspective with stunning panoramic views of the CBD and surrounding parks. The stacked topography of the sky gardens and sky pool recalls rice-patty terraces that can be found throughout Indonesia.

Rendering, residents' rooftop amenities

Rendering, residents' rooftop pool

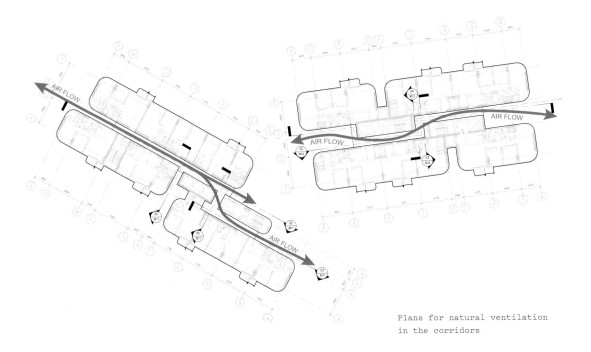

Plans for natural ventilation
in the corridors

Enlarged elevation of rooftop

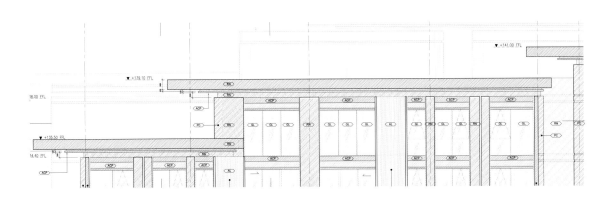

Rendering, pedestrian entrance

Model studies

China World Trade Center

Beijing, China
Status: Planning
GFA: 57,000 m² (614,000 ft²)
Site Area: 19,580 m² (210,760 ft²)
Building Height: 48 m (157 ft)

The China World Trade Center has grown organically over the past thirty years, and this will be the fifth and final phase of the development. Although it is highly visible and recognizable from a distance, when looking at the masterplan it is evident that there is neither a civic focal point nor a real entrance to the complex. Therefore this mixed-use scheme will be the missing link to unify the different components of the development.

The proposal looks at doing this by two complementary approaches. The first is to introduce a 'Civic Green' to benefit the entire masterplan. Second, the proposal is to develop a singular, powerful and obvious 'Front Door' to the entire complex, located at the most visible and accessible corner of the site. The new development will allow the basement to form a continuous 'Retail Loop', which also ties the current and future subway lines together. The intent is to enable and encourage connections over and under the Third Ring Road. As the new entrance to China World, 3C will become a kind of catalyst – a cultural centre that brings people together from within and also far beyond China World Trade Center.

The challenge of the scheme – and also its motivation – is to allow the Civic Green, the Front Door and the Retail Loop to complement each other, as they are seen as equally important. As the project is fundamentally a commercial development, a large portion of the site must be allocated to money-generating activities. Consequently, the Civic Green was lifted above ground level. However, it was also important that this green space did not just become an unseen green roof. To make the Civic Green viable, it has become a sloped plane which dips down to the main entrance and is immediately accessible and visible from all levels of the development.

Rendering, looking northwest

Diagram of the ice rink connections

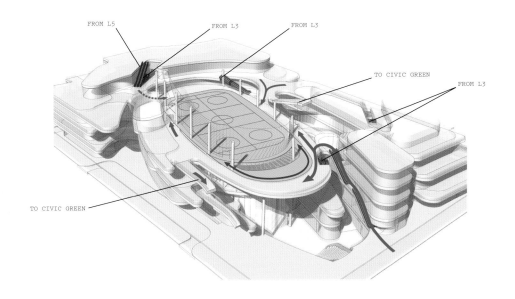

FROM L5

FROM L3

FROM L3

TO CIVIC GREEN

FROM L3

TO CIVIC GREEN

Rendering, looking west

Rendering, rooftop sledding hill in winter

Rendering, the café overlooking the ice rink

Rendering, the main circulation path

Exploded circulation diagram showing
vertical connections

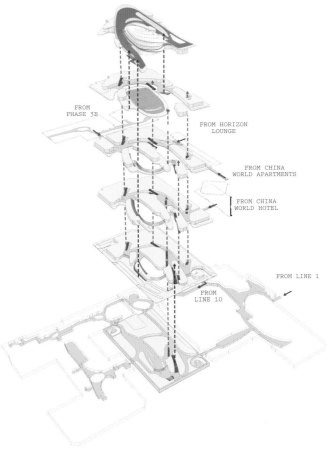

FROM
PHASE 3B

FROM HORIZON
LOUNGE

FROM CHINA
WORLD APARTMENTS

FROM CHINA
WORLD HOTEL

FROM LINE 1

FROM
LINE 10

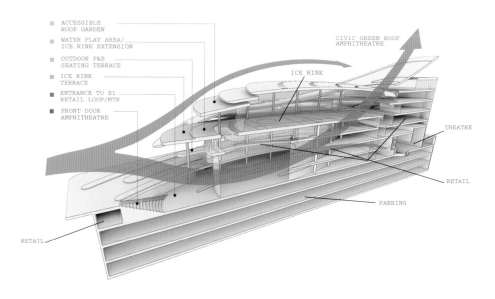

ACCESSIBLE
ROOF GARDEN

WATER PLAY AREA/
ICE RINK EXTENSION

OUTDOOR F&B
SEATING TERRACE

ICE RINK
TERRACE

ENTRANCE TO B1
RETAIL LOOP/MTR

FRONT DOOR
AMPHITHEATRE

CIVIC GREEN ROOF
AMPHITHEATRE

ICE RINK

THEATRE

RETAIL

PARKING

RETAIL

Sectional diagram

Rendering, looking west

The Commerce Centre

Brussels, Belgium
Status: Concept
GFA: 163,509 m² (1,759,996 ft²)
Site Area: 10,729 m² (115,486 ft²) (Phase 1),
10,874 m² (117,047 ft²) (Phase 2)
Building Height: 160 m (525 ft)

Located in the heart of Brussels, the Commerce Centre is a mixed-use project that is unique in Europe, both in scale and typology. The project replaces two existing blocks within a mature district in central Brussels. The aim was to develop a new node which would become a catalyst to re-energize the entire district as a vibrant, pedestrian-friendly environment.

The project benefits from close proximity to one of the city's main regional train stations, and is just across the river from the historic district of the city. The approach to the project was to 'book-end' the two sites with the major massing of the brief to define a large and inviting 'urban room' between them, visible from the main station. This room would then be activated through the location there of twenty-four-hour activities, including restaurants and bars, hotels, offices, residential properties and supporting retail units. These facilities are largely located on the lower levels to support the pedestrian activities. The areas account for about 25% of the more than 160,000 m² (1.7 million ft²) project, with the remaining areas being a mix of user-occupied and leasable office space.

Infused through the entire development are civic gestures encouraging interaction on multiple levels, from the street all the way into the tower's intermediate garden spaces and atria. All gestures are positioned to allow a blurring of programme uses, which encourage vitality throughout the day. The two book-ends then become a highly recognizable symbol from a distance, signifying the centre of this district.

Rendering, street level, Phase 1

Rendering, office tower atrium

Rendering, hotel atrium

Diagram model

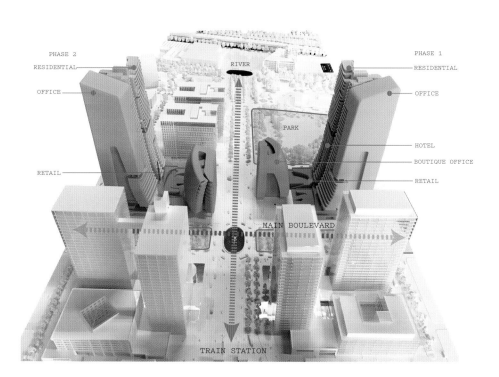

Diagram showing caverns

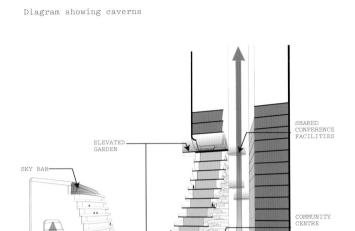

SKY BAR

ELEVATED
GARDEN

SHARED
CONFERENCE
FACILITIES

COMMUNITY
CENTRE

AMPHITHEATRE

Rendering, civic square

Rendering, view from the adjacent park

51

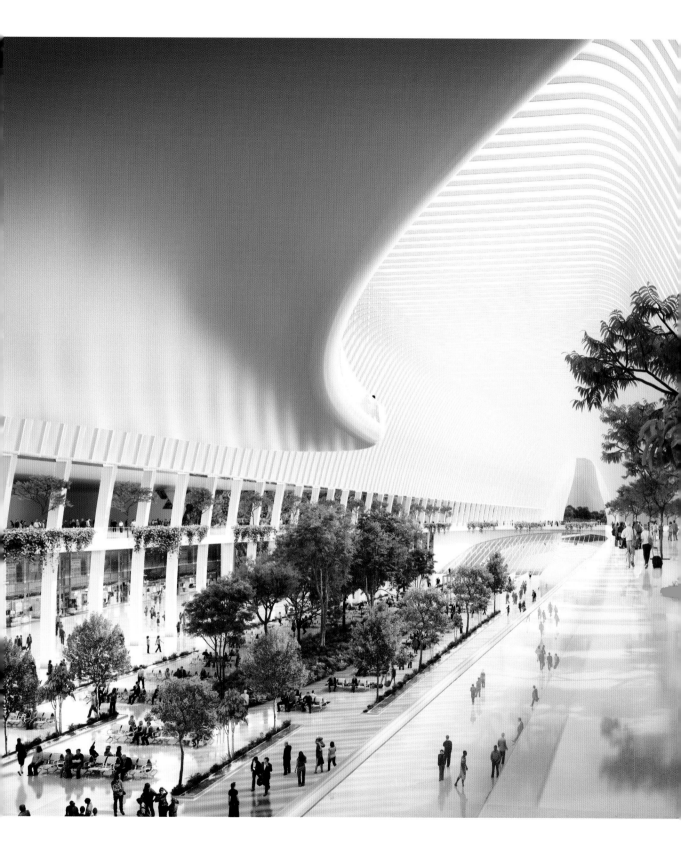

High Speed Rail

Southeast Asia
Status: Concept
GFA: 224,000 m² (2,411,116 ft²)
Site Area: 21,600 m² (232,500 ft²)
Building Height: 50 m (164 ft)

High Speed Rail is a terminus which connects two Southeast Asian countries. The station will contain arrival and departure immigration facilities for both countries. This was considered most efficient due to it being the only stop in the country it is located within, while connecting to multiple stations throughout the other country.

As a below-ground station, the design was focused on two concerns. The first of these was the arrival sequence through the lush vegetation surrounding the project. The second was the image and visibility of the station within its context.

The trains would go underground at the border of the country, and consideration was given to reconnecting with the natural air and light prior to entering the station. The landscape was carved away in front of the station, allowing the trains to be flooded with daylight on their approach, while the landscape opens up, giving views to surrounding tropical vegetation. This was an attempt to reduce the disorientation that can arise from being below ground for an extended period of time. It also provides a special and distinct gateway into the city, enabling better orientation.

The vegetation and natural airflow are taken into the station as an extension of the environment, allowing for immediate and direct natural wayfinding.

The station is presented outwardly as a series of vertical blades, which formally connects it to the surrounding forest; these are extended to a constant height. This provides a view of the actual length of the below-ground station, but also gives a point of reference to the surrounding 'hilly' topography. The main entrance is then discreetly cut into the hillside with a transition through the earth before re-emerging into this lush hidden valley connecting sky to tracks.

Rendering, station departure hall

Rendering, station ticket hall

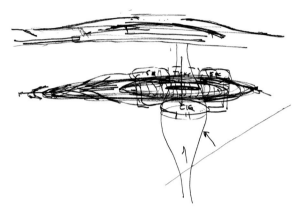

Sketches, section (top) and plan (bottom)

Rendering, looking towards the entrance

Rendering, roof extension

Rendering, aerial view

Cross-section sketch

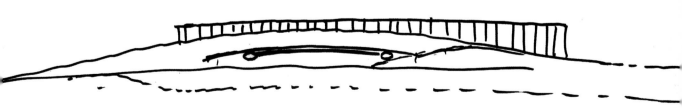

Elevation sketch

Integrated Hub

Undisclosed location, Southeast Asia
Status: Planning/on hold
GFA: 140,000 m² (1,507,000 ft²)
Site Area: 9,090 m² (97,844 ft²) (Parcel A),
26,703 m² (287,429 ft²) (Parcel B)
Building Height: 145 m (476 ft)

The Integrated Hub (IH) is the focal development in a vibrant regional district of a major Southeast Asian city centre. Defining the project as a 'mixed-use development' trivializes just how mixed the uses actually are. The project can be divided into four distinct typologies: an end-user office tower; regional transport, which includes a significant bus interchange; commercial uses of both office and retail; and civic uses, which consist of a library, a community centre and a sports centre.

The project strives to organize these varying typologies, harness the energy of the different user types, and intertwine them in an environment where boundaries are blurred and immersed in a lush natural landscape as a true urban park, which in itself becomes the fifth typology. The IH strives to find a new urban symbiotic landscape, showing how the built environment and nature may coexist together and ultimately provide a path forward, mitigating the detrimental effects of urbanization.

The project organizes the western edge adjacent to the busy road, with the commercial uses of the project and the tower anchoring it in the southwest corner. These uses are able to come down to the street level, helping to define a human-scale, articulated active edge to the IH.

The civic uses were then organized towards the east, away from the noise of the street, and positioned in an 'urban room' surrounded by residential developments. The challenge, however, was that this area had to be lifted off the ground over the bus interchange and over existing elevated train tracks. Above everything, and cascading down as terraces, is The Park, which is a truly public, highly vegetated and easily accessible 4.4-hectare (10.9-acre) green civic space.

The entrances to the library, the community centre and the sports centre are located 20 m (66 ft) above the ground and the train tracks. There are many vertical connections to these entrances at a nodal point of the outdoor wind canyons, which enables comfortable outdoor connections to be made across the site. Protected from the intense sun and tropical downpours, the canyons also facilitate cooling breezes, which enable the three civic programmes to exist within an elevated village carved into and coexisting with The Park.

Rendering, aerial view

+254.270 F. F. L. MEP ROOF

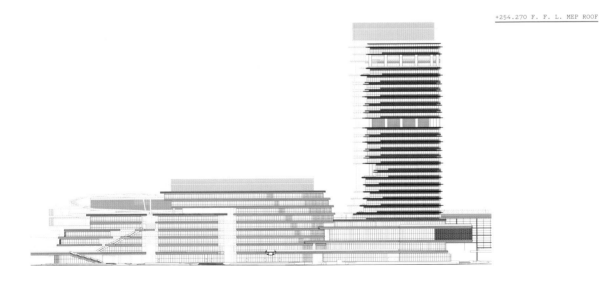

Elevation, tender drawing

Rendering, rooftop public park

Rendering, west elevation

Interior rendering, sports centre

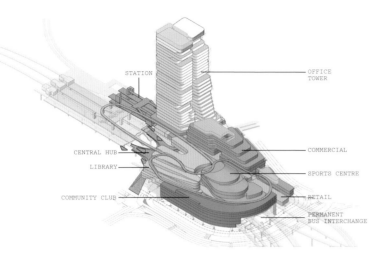

STATION

OFFICE TOWER

CENTRAL HUB

LIBRARY

COMMUNITY CLUB

COMMERCIAL

SPORTS CENTRE

RETAIL

PERMANENT BUS INTERCHANGE

Programme distribution diagram

Rendering, running track within park canyon

Rendering, aerial view looking west

Rendering, library reading room and atrium

Rendering, looking south adjacent to sports centre
OVERLEAF Rendering, looking south over
existing tracks

GUANGZHOU: RISING OUT OF THE MARSHES

If you are not taking a car from Hong Kong to Guangzhou, you cross over into Shenzhen, cross the border, and immediately rise above the ground on elevated road. The Guangzhuou-Shenzhen Expressway is a private toll road built to connect Hong Kong to Guangzhou (previously known in the West as Canton), the traditional centre of the Pearl River Delta, as well as the up-and-coming port city of Shenzhen. Factories, apartment blocks, remnants of swamps and mangrove forests, and expanses of water are framed by green hills. 'It's an amazing landscape,' comments Bromberg. 'You can see all the container ships going up there, and all the smaller boats, and all the harbour activity and then the factories and apartment buildings. But once you get past the silty flatness, you start to see these really green lush hills, a malleable landscape that you can imagine this water carving through, existing between these two different edges. It's easy to imagine thousands of years ago this clean valley that, every now and then, when the Pearl River flooded, became submerged all the way to where this low topography stops at the hills. Now we're looking at chaotic sprawl that's endless. There is nothing about this that gives you any sense of where you are or where you're going.'

Rome, Italy (2000), by Andrew Bromberg. Tension: the old built on to the ancient Teatro di Marcello.

In many ways the Pearl River Delta epitomizes what China, at least around the huge cities that cover more and more of its eastern seaboard, has become: an immense landscape of production held together, defined and marked by the arteries and nodes of mass movement. The airports, train stations, container ports and highway interchanges are its monuments, while the rivers, roads and train lines are its connective tissue. The Pearl River Delta was always China's interface with the West, and now it faces the world, as well as being the world's largest factory region.

Unlike the other cities that have been so vital to China's history and economy, located along the great rivers that run right across the country, Guangzhou is situated on a relatively short river and feels removed from the rest of the mainland. The river rises out of the Dayu and Nanling mountains, which arc around the delta and reach a height of almost 400 m (1,312 ft). It is an

'Now we're looking at a chaotic sprawl that's endless. There is nothing about this that gives you any sense of where you are or where you're going'

unusual geological formation, with the only close comparison being the Basque Mountains (Basque Arc) in the north of Spain. Though these mountains are neither tall nor impenetrable enough to completely cut off the delta from the mainland, they give the region its particular character and even a distinct climate.

Any delta benefits from a continual deposition of nutrients by the river on its way to the ocean, and on the Pearl River this agricultural bounty resulted in the development of ever larger cities, most notably Guangzhou. Over time these urban hubs became trading centres from which ships sailed, and which in turn received goods from all over the world. Hong Kong was a relative latecomer to this economic constellation, created by the British in the 18th century out of a fishing village. Similarly, starting in 1979, the Chinese government transformed another such hamlet, Shenzhen, into what is now an urban agglomeration home to almost ten million people. Together with Guangzhou, as well as Donggang and Foshan, themselves cities with millions of inhabitants, it forms a vast sprawl that now covers the entire valley almost as uniformly as the silt, mangrove forests and rice paddies that have traditionally been the defining landscape elements of the delta.

The Expressway weaves from Shenzhen to Guangzhou's suburbs almost completely on concrete pylons, with few exits. It was built between 1987 and 1997 by the Chinese-American billionaire Gordon Wu to facilitate rapid travel between the major metropolitan centres. Meanwhile the connections between the many villages and smaller towns in between are left to roads that must cross many tributaries and wind through dense population centres, as well as to the natural mode of transport here – boats. Only recently have the high-speed trains, which run throughout the day at almost full capacity every ten minutes between Shenzhen and Guangzhou, come to rival the highway for quick connectivity.

'I have been to some city parks in Guangzhou, and they are lovely. Great hills, virgin terrain, it's wonderful. You get a sense of what this landscape was like'

This is the workshop of the world, with a GDP (if you counted it as a country) of over $1.2 trillion and a population of over 100 million people. A mixture of housing and factories housing all that activity dominates the vistas from the raised Expressway. The scale is immense. 'Yeah, I stopped being amazed a long time ago at that scale,' Bromberg sighs in viewing the delta from the Expressway; 'maybe I shouldn't have.'

The road is part of that new continuity of concrete, as are the container ports in Hong Kong and Shenzhen, and the new bridges and tunnels that are part of the high-speed rail system. Yet all the apartment blocks and towers, the factories rising over many hectares, the roads and bridges connecting them all, the glass and steel skyscrapers bursting out of the traditional cores of the cities, are still as fragmented as the agricultural fields between the mangrove swamps, creeks, rills and rivers.

They are still overshadowed by the hills rising above all this, which, in turn, are overshadowed by the surrounding mountains and the mother river of the Pearl, so that the whole human-made landscape is still subject to nature in all its scale and variety of modes. However, this new reality threatens to become as powerful and coherent as what we see as the basic, default condition that frames our existence.

The delta's saving grace is its greenery. Shenzhen, which we think of as a factory town for its sheer scale and the speed of its development, appears above all else as a verdant metropolis, arching its way around Hong Kong Bay with waterfront parks, and stitched together with boulevards. Small parks dot the cityscape, while most of the new developments take the form of super-blocks made up of a few to a dozen high-rises, bordered by rows of shops and department stores, sometimes containing schools or other public institutions, but with whatever open space they have always covered with plants, trees and lawns.

Segesta, Sicily, Italy (1993), by Andrew Bromberg. Tension: the Greek temple of Segesta surrounded by farmland.

'I have been to some city parks in Guangzhou, and they are lovely,' Bromberg recalls. 'Great hills, virgin terrain, it's wonderful. You get a sense of what this landscape was like. But the amount of urbanization between them is incredibly dense. You can start to feel the pollution everywhere, and the smog everywhere. And then there is the river, and the green around it, and it just opens it all up.'

The scale of the water is what gives the delta its breadth. It is immense enough to have thwarted the building of a bridge

Hoi An, Vietnam (1997), by Andrew Bromberg. Tension: the
Japanese covered bridge connecting to a Chinese quarter
in Vietnam.

near its mouth until now (several are currently planned),
and connects you to the distant views out to the South China
Sea, where the water grows more expansive, reducing the land
to smaller and smaller islands that appear to be fragments
of the underlying geology swamped by the sheer volume of ocean.
It is that water that makes Hong Kong what it is, and that
draws the communities together, both economically and visually,
while also giving them a certain breathing room.

   As you leave the elevated Expressway to enter a spaghetti
of highways, the entry route into Guangzhou isn't necessarily
obvious until you encounter the scale and design of its core
along the Pearl River. The central business district is like
every other such accumulation of towers and blocks anywhere
in the world. A few signature spires, designed by the American
and European architectural companies you might expect (SOM, HOK,

KPF and DCM, to name just a few), distinguish Guangzhou from
similar cities, both close by and abroad. The civic centre is
more typically Chinese: a broad expense of a plaza, a congress
hall and then civic structures including a museum. Most striking
of all is the opera house, designed by the late Iraqi-British
architect Zaha Hadid, and opened in 2010.

Across the river is the new business district, centred
on the 604-m (1,981-ft) high observation tower designed by
Dutch firm Information Based Architecture, itself perhaps with
more in common with the newly grown cities of Asia and parts
of the former Soviet empire. There, the streets are broader,
the green recedes and the visitor feels ordered by the logic
of efficiency. These are blocks for buying and selling, trading
and organizing, as well as for storing the cars and the people
that make it all work.

There you will find Pazhou Island, a stretch of land between
the river and a canal. Starting in 2004, Guangzhou developed its
trade centre here, and now it has grown to become the largest
in China,
as well as one
of the largest
in the world.
Covering 1.3
million m²
(14 million
ft²), it
consists
of blocks
whose scale
is difficult
to gauge,
as they rise
up out of
expanses
of parking,
infrastructure
and roads that

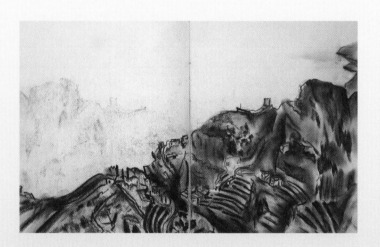

Below Ravello, Italy (1993), by Andrew Bromberg. Tension:
terraced lemon orchards warmed beneath black mesh canopies.

are themselves so broad that they defy measurement. This is the
emblem of all that Guangzhou has become. If the Pearl River Delta
is the workshop of the world, then this is its monument, both

the distillation of its activities of making and trading, and a memorial to the scale of the enterprise. And it is here that Bromberg has designed a mixed-used development containing a convention centre, office building and hotel.

His new facilities are located on two sites, but separated by 160 m (525 ft) by another parcel of land owned by a different developer. The project consists of several large halls that house trade shows, conventions and some retail, on top of which sit two mid-rise towers. Bromberg broke up the buildings' masses by slicing them into tubes, at least on the façade, each of whose ends he framed in angled concrete. Then, he pulled the towers apart: rather than being arranged vertically, they consist of tubes covered in tinted glass, stacked on top of each other and offset at slight angles, so that they seem to skip, cantilever and protrude in various directions. In both cases an atrium cuts through their middle, opening views up and down the inside, while emphasizing the fragmented nature of each of the two

Houseboat in Portage Bay, Seattle, USA (1995), by Andrew Bromberg. Tension: rippling waves and bobbing deck next to a motionless mooring post.

complexes totalling 160,000 m² (1,722,000 ft²).

'This site is on an island, with water flowing on both sides,' explains Bromberg, 'and I wanted you to feel as if the building had been shaped by being part of the delta. So, if you look at the lower exhibition centre, it is not malleable. The only thing I had to work with was pre-function areas, so those are what I pulled out and used to make this big mass appear to be more like boulders. The lower part of this building is the granite, that only gets partially formed by the water. The upper spaces, whether they are hotel rooms or offices in the other tower, are divorced from those restrictions. The two towers gesture towards each other, complete each other, so you get an electricity, that sort of jump between the two sites.'

'This site is on an island, with water flowing on both sides, and I wanted you to feel as if the building had been shaped by being part of the delta'

The geometries and the skins of glass tightly wrapped around what is happening inside these massive buildings might be abstracted natural forms: 'It might be a silly analogy, but since I felt I had less freedom with the pieces on the bottom, I saw them as that solid granite layer that withstands the flood waters and erosion.

Above is the sediment, which can be shaped a little bit more than the stone. So I wound up with a more or less solid podium, a tectonic plate. After the earth moves it creates vertical fractures, it shears away, so I put the fissures and cracks into it, while the top flows so much more.'

It is here that the challenge of responding to the site's natural conditions with a built form becomes most evident. Bromberg had originally foreseen a more open building, with the spaces between the various parts exposed to the climate, 'but the air is very dirty here, so we wound up enclosing the atriums'. Moreover, when considering future maintenance and cleaning costs in an environment with high levels of air pollution, the most logical way to skin a building of this scale in China is a curtain wall of glass and steel — so the architect cannot use the more obvious relation concrete has to solid masses of stone, let alone make buildings out of natural materials. The result is something that hints at conditions deep inside Bromberg's mind, and that he brings out in his drawings, but that have become somewhat more metaphorical in the building as it stands. Certainly, the structure is a beautiful composition of two fragments at an immense scale, made up of even more bits and pieces, gesturing to each other as they dance around their equally kinetic plinth.

The Nanfung Complex reacts most clearly to the human-made landscape, as is often the case with Bromberg's work. At its best, it activates and fragments the kind of programmes that usually result in stacks of floors clad in a more or less shaped skin. His offices and residential towers, in particular, undulate. They lean, bend, twist and curve. When faced with even larger programmes, he has a tendency to pull them apart into as many pieces as he can, breaking down their scale and creating complex visual relations between the pieces.

Bromberg's offices and residential towers, in particular, undulate. They lean, bend, twist and curve.

The effect of such strategies is not just to make his designs more human in scale and more pleasing to see, but also to turn them into mixers that dissolve the elements that together make up all the boxes around them. The complex doesn't just come apart or pixellate, but also poses a challenge to the behemoths across the way, offering them a mirror in which they are undressed or turned into partial skeletons, subverting their assumed coherence. If Bromberg's purest design ambitions are sometimes compromised by cost, construction practicalities and the preconceptions of clients and regulators, he certainly offers a riposte to the blandness that sometimes surrounds his constructions.

Bromberg talks about the places he envisioned opening vistas up and down, or to the outside, or where he aimed to emphasize the doors, where he designed a roof garden, or how he brings visitors into the convention floors in such a way that they will know where they are even in these caverns filled with purpose-built exhibition spaces. To that extent, it seems he is building for a third landscape: one beyond the physical, beyond the natural and the urban landscape. He is building in the world of regulations and codes: from the fire codes that tell him he can't have a slit the full height of a tower to prevent the spread of

Outside Atrani, Italy (1993), by Andrew Bromberg. Tension:
overgrown vegetation, steep hillsides and human-made terraces
for lemon trees.

flames, to the financial codes that tell him how much space
he needs, while other codes restrict the height of the buildings
or the expense of the materials, and structural calculations
tell him how far he can reach out in his gestures. Finally,
there are the more obscure codes that govern what an architect
can do before the client takes the commission away. The architect
must play a certain role, fulfilling the client's desires and
sense of self while also doing what they think is right as
the designer. Together these restrictions create a landscape
all their own, with narrow passages through which a project
must navigate to open new planes of possibilities. They shape
the building just as much as the wind, rain or sun.

   In this landscape Bromberg establishes his own language:
'Do I think how we as a society do our buildings is perfect for
what the world is? No. Do I believe I can go as far as I want to
go on every single project? Absolutely not. What I try to do very quickly is to understand the kind of comfort zone the client has. Then what I tell them every time is, 'I'm going to take you 10% past your comfort zone.' I know that there's a chance things will get pulled back. So right now, I always overshoot, knowing that aspects are going to get reeled

Varanasi, India (1995), by Andrew Bromberg. Tension:
populous western edge of the Ganges, with uninhabited
sandbanks to the east.

in. But I would rather do that than start off at fulfilling
expectations and try and push forward form there.' Perhaps that
is why his buildings are often so expressive and, to some people,
unconventional in their appearance. 'I like to think that I am
also responding to inner logic as well as the landscape in which
I am working, but I also have to find a way to place what I am
doing in such a way that the idea gets out, gets into shape.'

Bagan, Myanmar (2000), by Andrew Bromberg. Tension:
thousands of Buddhist temples and monuments interspersed
within green plains and farmland.

The view most visitors see of the Nanfung Complex is from
the rest of the convention complex. There is another view,
however. From across the canal to the south, the building has
a very different character. This is an older area, including
the neighbourhouds of Dawei and Dongyue, which was farmland
until the 1970s, when Guangzhou grew beyond the river, across
the island and into the countryside. It incorporated (or
subsumed) an existing village, and the area soon became part
of the continuous spread of construction that has since moved
miles further on to areas of new apartment blocks, shopping malls
and office buildings where there is still the order of newness.

This older neighbourhood is another world, a human-made
version of a mangrove forest. The buildings are closely packed,
some of them four to five storeys tall, while others are only

Udaipur, India (1995), by Andrew Bromberg. Tension: temples and
domes melding with trees and dissolving into Lake Pichola.

one or two storeys. People live above shops that spill out on to the pavements, where their wares and café chairs join stalls and groupings of people chatting or trading. The scale is small, the variations and colours many. Plaster covers apartments, while corrugated metal leans together to create a garage. Blue, orange and red paint and signs, plastic that is smooth and worn, clothes lines and satellite dishes, cars, minibuses and bicycles all mix together. It is not particularly beautiful and not organized, but it has a life of its own.

From a tree-lined promenade alongside the canal, the water's colour the same grey-brown as the smoggy sky, you can make out Bromberg's Nanfung Complex, a complete contrast. It looks beautiful from this perspective: a solid, angled base that seems to stand against the tide, while the glass tubes above it shift dimensions as the clouds move across the sky and reflections from the traffic highlight particular corners. The building floats and shimmers in a way that is not obvious from within its shadow.

Here there is no such thing as a human-made or a natural landscape, but rather a set of scenes, a collage of daily human activities

On this side of the canal are fishermen and couples, a mother with a pushchair, an old woman who seems lost in thought, far removed from what lies across the river. Here there is no such thing as a human-made or a natural landscape, but rather a set of scenes, a collage of daily human activities. Architecture and its setting, the making of monuments, is someplace else, someplace not accessible from here. Then, a sudden barrier, beyond which a continuous field of brick and broken concrete stretches out into the distance. New buildings appear, covered in glass, their function not yet clear. All that is apparent is that they are new, that they all look more or less the same, marching across the empty space the demolition crew has prepared for them. A construction crew is busy on the latest of them already, closer than the ones that look as if they have just been completed.

'This time next year, all this will be gone,' Bromberg says. He admits to a certain ambivalence about the development. The Dawei neighbourhood and its romantic walkway by the canal have a life and energy that is completely lacking in the area where he constructed his convention centre. Yet it is also dirty, packed and looks poor. What is more, he is dedicated to designing the kind of large buildings that will soon replace this scene. He consoles himself by believing that should he ever receive a commission to build here, his design would respond to the urban context and inhabitants that once occupied these spaces to make a new, third kind of landscape from the rubble of the past.

'Tension: increasing awareness of context, scale and time periods – adding richness to what are often homogeneous environments; a celebration of difference'

Nanfung Commercial, Hospitality and Exhibition Complex

Guangzhou, China
Status: Built (2013)
GFA: 161,780 m² (1,741,385 ft²)
Site Area: 2,525 m² (27,179 ft²)
Building Height: 123 m (404 ft)

Located outside Guangzhou on Pazhou Island, which is dedicated to exhibition-related activities, the Nanfung Commercial, Hospitality and Exhibition Complex contains four distinct programmatic uses split across two different sites, namely '1301' and '1401'. The complex is located opposite the government-funded exhibition centre that currently ranks as the second largest in the world, which presented considerable design challenges. This complexity became even more apparent with the realization that the sites of the project are 160 m (525 ft) apart, separated from each other by another building. The introduction of four primary uses to the complex was intended to diversify its offering and create a mixed-use vibrancy, with the aim of raising competitiveness and giving it a stronger chance of success.

'1301', also known as the Guangzhou Commercial Showcase Complex, houses a retail exhibition area in the podium with an office showroom building on top, while '1401', the Guangzhou Nanfung International Convention and Exhibition Centre/ Langham Place, is a traditional, multi-storey exhibition centre in the podium with a 500-room five-star hotel on top. Altogether the complex provides a gross floor area of more than 160,000 m² (1.7 million ft²).

The project design balanced the importance of 'frontage' for the visibility of the complex with basic functional constraints, including pedestrian flow, traffic flow, vehicular drop-offs and appropriate areas for loading/unloading zones. This was formalized into a simple functional diagram, which enables the achievement of very efficient area layouts.

The primary formal drivers for the design, however, are its contextual responses to the surrounding area as well as the physical separation of the two project sites. Contextually the project, which initially seems large, is fragmented in comparison to its surrounding dominant neighbours. Consequently, urban design restrictions placed strong emphasis on the podiums by requiring a simple and consistent presence on the major street wall to the north. The major entrances for the two sites are on the west side for '1301' and the east side for '1401'. These faces are where more articulation and playfulness in the podium exteriors were allowed and explored.

South elevations, site 1301 (left) and site 1401

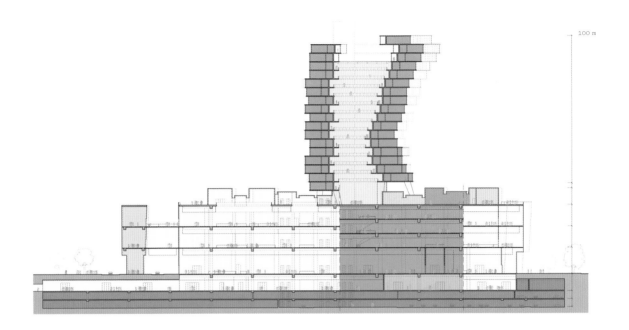

North/south section concept, site 1401

Site 1301, looking east

Competition model, with site 1401 to the left

Site 1301, podium rooftop looking west

Site 1301, looking east

Hotel atrium, site 1401

Hotel lobby

Ocean Heights

Dubai, United Arab Emirates
Status: Built (2011)
GFA: 87,940 m² (946,578 ft²)
Site Area: 3,746 m² (40,322 ft²)
Building Height: 310 m (1,017 ft)

Ocean Heights, a residential tower, is located in the prestigious Dubai Marina development. The eighty-two-storey structure makes an immediate visual impact through a combination of soaring height and the intriguing geometry of its form. Its essence lies in the unexpected 'twist' three of its faces take as they rise from the building's base. No mere affectation, Ocean Heights I's defining feature evolved from a need to offer ocean vistas for as many of its units as possible. Thanks to the 'twist' – and the structure's orientation away from the orthogonal grid and towards one of Dubai's Palm Islands – even units at the rear of the structure now enjoy an attractive view of the sea beyond.

Adding to the design challenge of Ocean Heights was the client's strict need for consistent layouts for the residential units. To achieve this within the building's sinuous envelope, the architects developed a strongly rationalized – and surprisingly simple – system of standard 4-m (13-ft) wide modules. These track their way down the building, with only the façade component of each subtly changing to form the contours of the exterior. In another unusual touch, Ocean Heights' sheer walls were placed perpendicular to the mean of the two most extreme angles of the façade. By doing this, the architects were able to 'soften' the relationship between the façade and partitions, thereby minimizing how 'off-perpendicular' the relationship becomes.

With Ocean Heights gathering accolades even before its completion – the project received the Bentley 'Best Architecture' award in 2006 – it was only natural that the same client should continue their winning partnership with Aedas with an even more stunning follow-up. The result was DAMAC Heights.

Northwest elevation (right), looking over the Persian Gulf

Cross-section

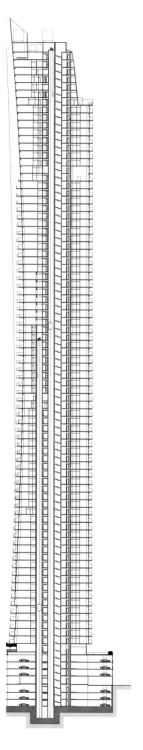

TOP OF FIN LVL
+310.00

Slot in southwest façade, looking up

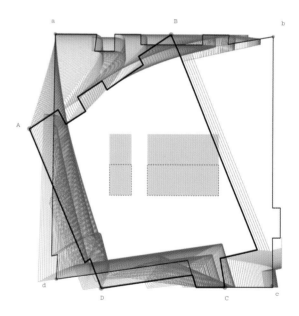

Overlaid plans setting out the geometry
of the tower

The tower's southwest façade

The tower's northwest façade

Axonometric plan and geometry study

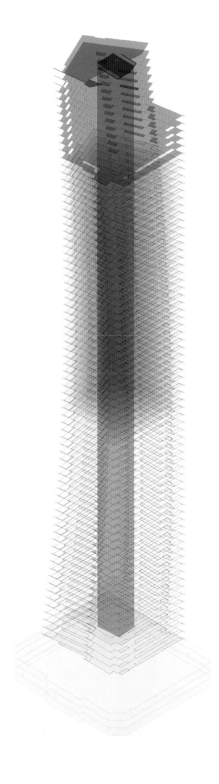

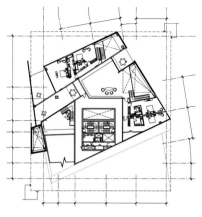

81st floor plan

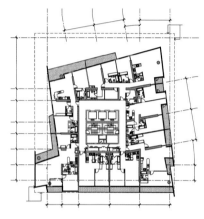

46th floor plan

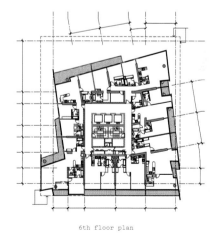

6th floor plan

Daxing Xihongmen Mixed-use Development

Beijing, China
Status: Construction (Phase 1 - 2017, Phase 2 - 2020)
GFA: 610,268 m² (6,568,870 ft²)
Site Area: 121,010 m² (1,302,541 ft²)
Building Height: 80 m (262 ft)

Located off of the Fifth Ring Road in southeast Beijing, the Daxing Xihongmen Mixed-use Development is intended to be the anchor project for a future retail centre in Beijing. The site is located at the southern edge of the district, fronting a new urban green corridor. The project, which consists of 150,000 m² (1.6 million ft²) of retail, 180,000 m² (1.9 million ft²) of offices and 35,000 m² (377,000 ft²) of hotel, strives to serve as a stitch in the urban fabric with the green space to the south, as well as a commercial threshold to the retail centre to the north. The site is split into two plots, and utilizes a common language to unify the development, which consists of office towers in the west and a more horizontal retail programme to the east.

Formally, the project plays with north/south striated, geological forms which emerge out of the landscape to the south while forming a more defined urban edge on the north. The strong geometric striations allow for porosity within the development while breaking down the larger massing to create various access points, which encourages engagement with the adjacent site occupants. As a result the plot links the two adjacent sites, facilitating continuity between the existing northern retail and southern park space.

The strongly formal, directional gesture recalls the natural erosion of stones within a riverbed, as the edges of the development smooth out and expose its interior components. Finally, the eroded mass dissolves completely towards the south, allowing for a public park space which relates to the existing adjacent southern park as a continuation of its greenery and paths that seem to pull at the development.

Rendering, looking northeast

Ground floor plan showing site connectivity

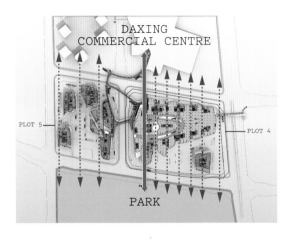

Street view, looking northeast

Detailed view, looking west

Concept image

Rendering, detail, looking west

Rendering, park view, looking north

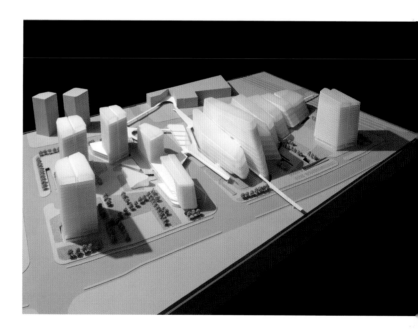

Concept model, looking northeast

Plac Grzybowski

Warsaw, Poland
Status: Planning/on hold
GFA: 42,848 m² (461,212 ft²)
Site Area: 4,181 m² (45,004 ft²)
Building Height: 120 m (394 ft)

Located in the heart of Warsaw, within the historic Grzybowski Square, Plac Grzybowski is a non-traditional mixed-use project positioned as connector between old and new, between history and the future, between majority and minority, between discrimination and acceptance, and ultimately between the city of Warsaw and the Jewish population.

The land on the square is currently owned by one Jewish group, and contains an existing Jewish theatre operated by a different Jewish group.

The Ministry of Culture is a partner in the 300-seat theatre, and understands the importance the theatre has played in Poland as the only continuation of a culture that was close to extinction following the travesties of the Holocaust. The landowner, as a non-profit foundation, lacks the funds necessary to bring the fifty-year-old theatre up to modern legislative and performance requirements. Consequently, it approached Ghelamco, a Belgian developer, to become its partner in building a new theatre and its office headquarters, with the costs offset by including a 30,000 m² (323,000 ft²) speculative office tower as part of the scheme.

Early on, however, the important role the project can play in 'mending' and 'merging' different events surrounding the site became apparent. The new theatre is designed to be open, visible and inviting. The site itself, located on the city's historic square, which was within the Warsaw Ghetto, is also directly between Warsaw's cathedral and the only synagogue to survive the Second World War. The theatre becomes a symbolic connection, reflecting the current harmony of modern Warsaw. The foyer of the theatre also forms a public connection between the church, the square and the synagogue, which also functions as a museum of the history of Grzybowski Square and the importance it has played in Warsaw's evolution.

The tower quickly evolved to become a sculptural expression and extension of the spirit of the Jewish theatre. Its articulation is optimistic and forward-looking, reaching for the future. The expression 'bent but not broken' here becomes a symbol of respect for what the Jewish people had to endure; they never lost their faith nor their pride in their culture and heritage.

Photomontage of Grzybowski Square, looking south

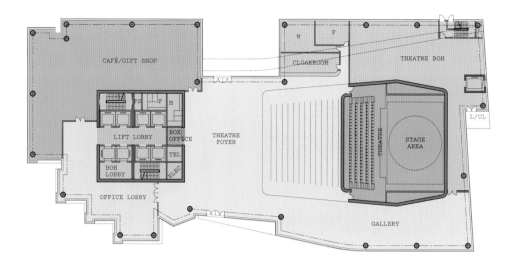

Ground floor plan

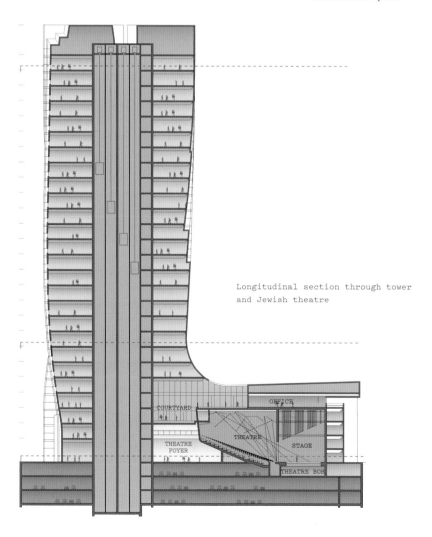

Longitudinal section through tower
and Jewish theatre

Rendering, west façade over Grzybowski Square

ALL SAINTS CHURCH   THEATRE FOYER   NOZYK SYNAGOGUE

Foyer concept, connection between church
and synagogue

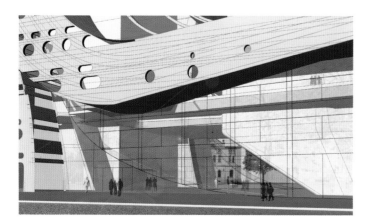

Study for main entrance

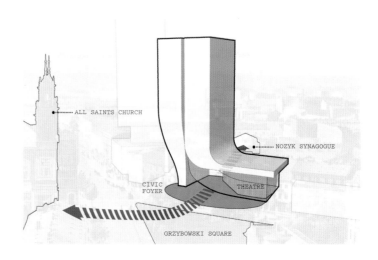

ALL SAINTS CHURCH   NOZYK SYNAGOGUE

CIVIC
FOYER   THEATRE

GRZYBOWSKI SQUARE

Concept, connection between church
and synagogue

"BENT BUT NOT BROKEN"

Design concept, Jewish culture in Poland

Rendering, Jewish theatre off Grzybowski Square

Cloud on Terrace

Shanghai, China
Status: Construction (2021)
GFA: 45,000 m² (484,000 ft²)
Site Area: 11,647 m² (125,367 ft²)
Building Height: 99.6 m (327 ft)

Cloud on Terrace is located near the historic Changde Road, close to two metro stations and a planned future green area in the southern residential zone. The project consists of an office tower and a retail podium. The project had the additional challenge of requiring a bridge between the low-rise, residential developments to the south and Changshou Road to the north.

The tower is set back from the retail at the property edge, with lush terraces acting as an extension of the green park to the south. Entrances to the retail are visible at both ends, facing the busy pedestrian junctions and connecting the two metro station entrances. The lower portion is highly accessible, bringing a humanism that had been missing from the urban fabric. The tower itself was deliberately ambiguous, with the soft forms appearing to dissolve both into the surroundings and the sky above. Its form and articulation were intended to enable the tower to 'float' above the green terraces of the retail below as a cloud might seem to hover or sit on a hill.

The tower's placement and angular orientation are a deliberate result of optimizing open views, creating a visible form along Changshou Road. To further direct the building's energy towards this important main street, the curtain-wall façade of the front face gently ripples towards the top, further dissolving the form and softening its reflections of the surroundings.

A recessed 'cave' below breaks down the mass to a pedestrian scale and allows the terraces to extend up into the tower. Tight horizontal extrusions open up towards the south as sunshades, reducing solar gain into office floors. The curtain wall uses high-performance, energy-saving, low-emissivity, low-iron glass. The natural landscaping on the podium terrace balconies also reduces solar gain into the project and maximizes the green on site to give a naturally ventilated environment.

Rendering, tower interface, looking north

Tender drawing, façade detail section

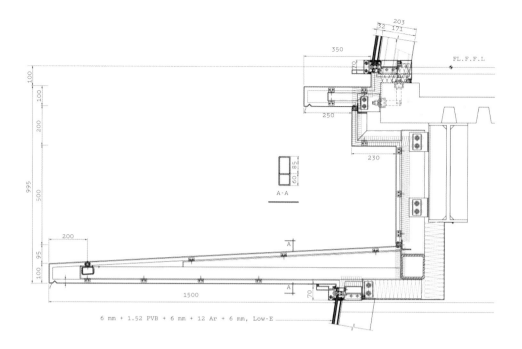

A-A

6 mm + 1.52 PVB + 6 mm + 12 Ar + 6 mm, Low-E

North elevation

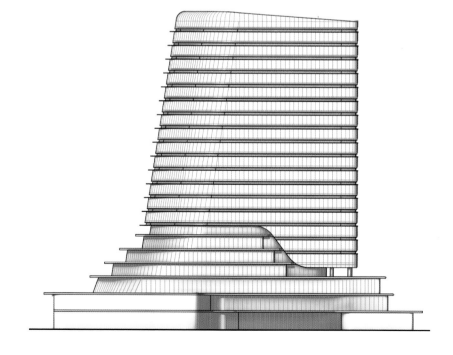

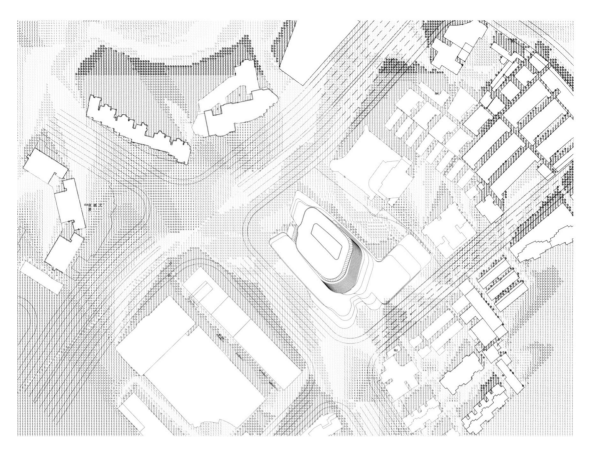

Shadow casting analysis

3D-printed model studies
OVERLEAF North façade from primary boulevard

SINGAPORE: GOING WITH THE FLOW

Like Hong Kong, Singapore is an island. However, it is a very
different type of island. If the former is dominated by its
Peak, craggy and abrupt in its vertical rise, then the latter
presents a low, soft and smooth terrain; Singapore spreads
rather than rises. If Hong Kong is no longer just an island,
but rather a collection of urban nodes that spread north between
the mountains, up through the Pearl River Delta, then Singapore
is still very much on its own, its back turned on Malaysia,
the country of which it was once part and on which it still
depends for such crucial resources as water. And if Hong Kong
is a landscape of competition between peaks and towers, and
among the towers themselves, then Singapore is a place of
planned continuity that seems to swell up as slowly as its
hills. Everything flows in Singapore, including Andrew
Bromberg's buildings.

Singapore is both a human-made and a natural quasi-Eden.
Because it is an island, its tropical climate not only harbours
a lush vegetation in which Adam and Eve might have been quite
at home, but it is also almost always breezy and slightly
cooler than inland areas nearby. As an island, the city-state is
isolated, and its strict
government has been able
to completely control
its environment to
promote that flow.
It plans and controls
how many cars are
licensed, and uses
a complex mechanism
of permits and charges
to remove the potential
for congestion. The
result is homogeneity
and an almost narcotic
atmosphere that works
well enough to have
become a desirable

Inle Lake, Myanmar (2000), by Andrew Bromberg. Shelter: stilt
houses raised above the flood plains.

model for cities around the world.

This dedication to planning means that there is an inherent
logic and, in most cases, a sense of 'rightness' about how
the island has developed. The older part of downtown, the part

of the city that Singapore's Urban Redevelopment Authority (URA) has worked hard to preserve, offers lessons for how to create a walkable and varied urban streetscape. Walking under arched promenades that provide protection from the summer sun while the buildings rise up all around, Bromberg observes, 'These walking arcades protect you from the light and also the tropical rain that is such a big part of this place. You're in these sidewalks, not under the sun, the breeze is coming through. You're able to walk for these very long blocks,

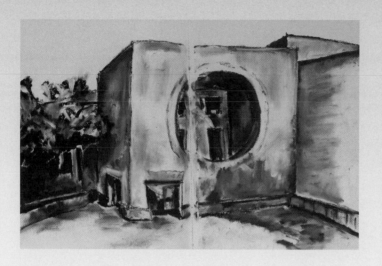

Indian Institute of Management, Ahmedabad, India (1995), by Andrew Bromberg. Shelter: deep, shaded relief from the scorching desert climate.

not crossing streets very often. The street itself is very thin, so you can imagine that during a really dense rainstorm, it's just a quick jump across the street and you're protected again.' A big part of what makes these narrow streets and pavements work is that the blocks consist of what are called 'shophouses' – structures with a narrow face on the front for retail visibility, a store that reaches back to the centre of the block, then a courtyard or courtyards and the housing for the storekeeper and their family beyond that. As Bromberg points out, 'They're so deep and the store frontage is very small, so you actually get a lot of variety on every block. It's not the traditional retail model where you get huge frontage, but instead you feel as if you are continually seeing something new and different.'

It is the starting point for Singapore's fabric. It is not the way the city developed later, as the logic of capitalism says such units are far too small to make sense as a city grows.

The Forbidden City, Beijing, China (2001), by Andrew Bromberg.
Shelter: many layers of insulation and transition from public to
private domains.

Singapore became a city of office towers in its heart, shopping malls reaching towards the centre of the island, and all around seas of apartment blocks, which range from the repetitive ranks of residential units the government built to guarantee housing for all, to the pencil-thin high-rises where the wealthy live in splendid isolation.

What is distinct in Singapore is both the arrangement of the pieces and the texture of the overall place

This much is not so different from most Asian cities that have developed in the last few decades, but what is distinct in Singapore is both the arrangement of the pieces and the texture of the overall place. The city was first laid on top of and used to connect the small fishing villages and market places by the British, who imposed a grid on the downtown area. They also set the tone for residential developments with brick structures (the grander ones covered with stucco) accented with white-painted wood columns and pediments. Open spaces were connected with shaded allées. The whole was a tropical version of the kind of colonial settlement you can see around the world, from the United States to South Africa.

After the city-state's independence in 1965, the government adapted the various planning documents that had been drafted in the period after the Second World War, replacing them, in 1971, with the Concept Plan. This document, created with input from American, British and Dutch consultants, moved beyond standard methods of planning, such as zoning and infrastructure orientation, to think of the island's landscapes as a whole. Analogous to what the Dutch called 'spatial planning', the tools for this effort consisted of a concentration of integrated and multi-use zoning in a 'ring and line' belt of nodes surrounding a preserved centre, which would act as a water catchment area and public park. The traditional core would remain the control and administrative centre, and would grow out into the sea, not into the green area separating it from the new development areas. Transportation infrastructure, from the large scale (airport and port) to roads and rapid transit, coupled with a strategy of preserving historic neighbourhoods, would reinforce this idea of an island-wide Garden City.

As a result, Singapore now consists of a colonial core (the shophouses) elaborated into a dense web of shops and residences,

Recent awareness of the need for sustainability is bringing permeable, semi-public spaces back to the downtown area

a gridded downtown that is expanding on to a vast territory of flat sand that the Dutch engineering firms created out of the sea to the south, and pockets of development that ring the island's elevated and preserved core and are connected by roads and mass transit lines.

The central downtown district has developed just to the west of the Singapore River, across from the original colonial core, complete with its cricket grounds and Raffles Hotel. From there, streets lead towards the island's middle, following the contours of what is essentially one large hill made up of a series of subsidiary rises. The most famous of these streets, Orchard Road, turns into a parade of shopping malls that once drew visitors from all over Asia. As the roads move up into what are essentially the suburbs, they thin out and become less dense, but in the wealthier areas slender residential towers create a vertical counterpoint to the horizontal spread.

As the population grew and development progressed, the government encouraged something like the settlement patterns in Hong Kong: areas of high-rises grouped around mass transit systems. What is different in Singapore is that the towers for many years subsidized housing, as the government promised apartments to everybody. In recent years, the market has taken over, but the URA has encouraged strong design moves, such as the Interlace, designed by Büro Ole Scheeren and the Office for Metropolitan Architecture (OMA) as an elegant stack of giant pick-up sticks perched on a hillside. Social planning has given way to good design for the rich, but the pattern for

the fabric of what amounts to urban forest set within the
semi-tropical actual forests remains in place. The centre of
the island, meanwhile, has remained a nature preserve and water
catchment area.

Even more remarkable is the quality of many of the large
buildings at ground level. Starting in the 1950s, when air-
conditioning was still a luxury, many office and shop buildings
would leave their first few floors open, often with one or more
courtyards in the middle. The arrangement encouraged breezes
to move through the whole building and up to the top, providing
natural ventilation. Over time, many developers and architects
abandoned that principle, but the recent awareness of the need
for sustainability is bringing such permeable, semi-public spaces
back to the downtown area.

Venturing across downtown Singapore and the river, you
encounter shops and restaurants spilling on to the pavements.
The river leads down to a basin created by the building of a new
piece of land projected to be six times as large as the current
downtown. Reaching far into the ocean, this is meant to be
a mixed-use peninsula, which will be larger than Manhattan,
and will be Singapore's pride and joy. While the first part of
it has been laid out
in a cookie-cutter
grid, some of the next
phases will attempt
to create new versions
of the mangrove swamps
that lined the original
shore, reflected in a
greater variety in the
street patterns.

Outside Mandalay, Myanmar (2000), by Andrew Bromberg.
Shelter: monastery lifted off the ground to allow ventilation
through the floor.

Here you can find
what has become the
island's signature:
three fifty-storey
slabs, each sliced down
the middle and sloping
outwards, connected
at the top by a 'skybridge'. It is a technical feat, and Bromberg
points out how much the architect, Moshe Safdie, built on
Singapore's traditions: 'It might be a closed building,

but notice how it opens up at the bottom, and look at how it spills down into a shopping mall by the bay, so that it stays connected to the water. The ground floor plan has a minimum amount of obstructions so that you're always able to see out and see the sky and the green. I think Moshe did a decent job of trying to soften the negative impact of it. You don't have the filigree, you don't have things that activate the plaza, so what you need is a large amount of people who spill out, and the scale of the whole collection of hotels, casino and shopping mall is such that it works.'

Bromberg's contributions to Singapore's recent developments have been in one of the more remarkable ex-urban nodes on the island. Called One North, it was masterplanned by the late architect Zaha Hadid. Instead of being made up of high-rises of a generic type, it consists of a pattern of teardrop-shaped plots that, when

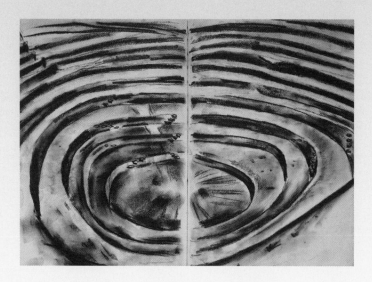

Corn terraces in Moray, Peru (1999), by Andrew Bromberg.
Shelter: experimental Inca terraces to optimize corn agriculture by elevation and the position of the sun.

you see the whole development in plan, seem to be sliding down a hill. Instead of replacing the natural setting, Hadid sought to create a form that reshaped it into something recalling the way water courses down a hill, or how the mangroves dissolve the line between land and water. She then decreed that developers must abide by height limits that varied with each lot, so that the area would build up to a higher core from sides that sought to respond to existing, colonial-era housing and other low-rise structures. Bromberg describes it as 'one sexy masterplan'.

He also points out that Hadid's plan promotes the permeability of the ground plane, encouraging the buildings to flow and open up to each other: 'They didn't shape the bottom, but they did allow the bottom to remain open and gave you certain benefits, like more square feet to develop, to have that happen. Which is great because she probably wanted to have that undulating topography.'

Bromberg's design in that context, for the Asian offices of Lucasfilm, George Lucas's animation company, as well as now for Lucasfilm's parent company, Disney, is called the Sandcrawler because of its resemblance to the lumbering, zoomorphic tank of the same name in the *Star Wars* films. Clad in slick, angular glass planes, it consists of two wings, curved at their back and angled towards the side. The fronts protrude from the protective cloak of the semi-reflective skin, revealing parts of the structure, over which plants spill from window boxes. The building may resemble a machine of war from some angles, but mostly it is simply glass, columns and lintels emerging out of nature, reflecting even more of the landscape.

Bromberg has turned the whole base into a sloping bit of jungle park open to the public and extending through the Sandcrawler's heart. 'We wanted the building to be as accessible to the public as possible. At the same time we realized that confidential animations are happening here, and everyone is going to try and get a sneak peek of those things. So, we lifted the building off the ground, to keep things separate that need to be. That move allows us to have this park, which is pretty inviting. They actually buried a Yoda down there, and it's one of the most attractive elements of the park. Everyone wants to try and find the Yoda buried in this overgrown garden.'

To wander through the ground floor of cool and shaded colonnades, out into the jungle, and to look up at the office floors gives you the impression that, at least in Singapore, architecture could be fragments of inhabitation, shards of containment and pieces of technology growing out of the landscape, creating their own moments of what the Germans call 'office landscapes'. Here the term comes close to reality, as Bromberg has brought vegetation into the upper floors and opened up the prow to allow visitors to experience the undulating natural and Hadid-planned landscape.

On the other side of One North, Bromberg has designed an altogether more open building: the Star. After following the snaking paths – manicured and miniaturized versions of Singapore's boulevards – up through a park at the development's highest point, back down again and around a corner, the Star comes into view: a U-shaped construction of white metal and glass, hovering over terraced layers on tall, white columns. An explosion of forms balancing over a human-made landscape, it is a bold statement of Bromberg's design principles and architectural bravura.

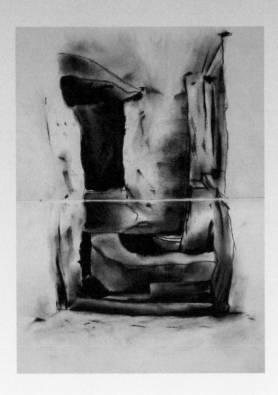

Atrani, Italy (1993), by Andrew Bromberg. Shelter: well inside an old farmhouse.

The Star was developed by a consortium of Capitaland and Rock Productions, which is owned by the New Creation Church. Capitaland owns and operates the lower retail floors, while Rock Productions owns and operates the upper civic and cultural components above. The New Creation Church rents out the facility on Sundays to house its services, which regularly fill the 5,000-seat theatre to capacity several times over on Sundays, while many more around the world watch its highly choreographed rituals, musical performances and sermons. Singapore does not allow churches to be that large or prominent, so although the building is used by the church, it is designed as a state-of-the-art performance space for rock and roll shows, musicals and revues, and just happens to also host religious ceremonies one day a week. Capitaland Corporation, the island's largest developer, planned shopping and dining areas (predominantly the latter) for the Star to cater to the occupants of One North, commuters from the nearby mass transit stop, and the visitors to the performances described above.

Bromberg was lucky enough to encounter a programme that was ripe for the creation of contrasting landscapes, and he was smart enough to make the most of these conditions. The easiest thing to do would have been to either sink the theatre into the ground and cover it with the shopping, or to place it directly on top of the shopping. By separating the two chunks of building, Bromberg was able to give each of them a clear identity, while allowing most of the public spaces to be outdoors but shaded. The path up to the auditorium, either on escalators that pierce the Star's heart or up staircases that wind their way up part of the structure, leads past terraces and balconies, some of them shaped as outdoor amphitheatres or performance spaces, where visitors can rest and gather.

Bromberg has designed a vertical landscape that encourages movement and occupation. When visitors first arrive, they can follow a staircase and escalators that spill down into the ground, following gravity and the attraction of a central courtyard that is cool and sheltered. As people move up, past the undulating lines of stores and restaurants, they can look out over the surroundings as breezes follow those same contours and provide relief from the heat. The auditorium always looms above, sheltering you yet drawing you skyward. 'Beyond the shopping area we also wanted spaces to hang out and chill,' explains Bromberg. 'We looked at how to create an environment that allowed you to escape the heat, like in a cave. The lower portion of the Star is porous, to try to capture breezes and induce wind currents. The depression at

Bromberg was lucky enough to encounter a programme that was ripe for the creation of contrasting landscapes, and he was smart enough to make the most of these conditions

the base was an opportunity to allow leaked air-conditioned air to be used on the outside.'

As you rise towards that destination, you become increasingly aware of the building's structure, whose canted columns and beams sail past you on the escalators. You move into the realm where human-made forms assert themselves with all the angularity, juxtapositions and layering of spaces of which architecture is capable. The building becomes a ride in which you are introduced to the spectacle of design, which in turn serves to frame your views of the outside, while providing places for gathering and activity. When you arrive at the first lobby area, you are still outside, looking both down at the landscape you have just left and up at the artificial world controlled by the church. From there you move further up into the theatre itself, a deep and wide space where form gives way to another kind of spectacle created by the electronic wizardry of theatrical lighting and sound amplification, which transforms human actions into something altogether artificial (or perhaps otherworldly, if you are a believer).

Bromberg had at least one more chance to contribute to his version of Singapore. In 2016, he won the competition to design a mixed-use complex anchored by HQ offices for the island's mass transit authority, LTA, just a few miles away from One North. Right now the site is a vast field where the sun beats down on picnickers and football players, while buses and trains jam together in an overcrowded transit hub next door and shopping malls watch over the whole place. Bromberg's plan was to combine all these elements into a single structure that will include a transit interchange, reintroducing the flow so central to Singapore's smooth character, surrounded by shopping and surmounted by towers. Nature would flow around the whole base, creating the impression that the building (at least up to the towers) is a Hanging Gardens of Babylon-type structure: 'The whole landscape would be kind of floating in the sky. The bottom of the open spaces would be 20 m (66 ft) off the ground. We had to do it in this way because below this will be occupied by a bus interchange and rail lines. We were afraid that putting all of those spaces with buses moving around and would completely negate the kind of opening of the ground plane that we achieved at both the Sandcrawler and the Star. So what we tried to do was replace that lost landscape by putting it up on top. It will be a building floating above a sea of inaccessible uses, with a green, lush park space growing on top of that. It's a different model than the other two buildings, but with a similar goal.'

The architect imagined escalators and stairs that will bring people from both the outside and the bus and train station up past the shopping areas and through Singapore National Library, Singapore Sport and Singapore Community Centre, into a small forest, complete with streams, clearings and pools, shaded by the trees and the human-made mountains of LTA's headquarters tower that would rise up from here. It would have been his own version of the Singaporean forest. Unfortunately, the LTA cancelled the project at the end of 2017.

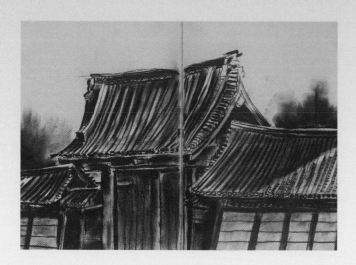

Kyoto, Japan (1999), by Andrew Bromberg. Shelter: main entrance and wall outside the Kyoto Gosho (Imperial Palace).

Much of that landscape remains, if not completely intact, at least preserved enough that visitors get a sense of what the place might have looked like before all the artificial spaces began to appear. The MacRitchie Reservoir Park, beyond residential developments and sports fields, offers a glimpse into the forests that once covered the island. Although today it looks ancient, it is actually a second-growth replanting after the area was cleared in the 19th century for agriculture. Within the reserve, tree roots crisscross the paths, their crowns meeting to provide continuous protection from the sun. 'Forests are amazing,' comments Bromberg, recalling his early days living in the shadows of the Rocky Mountains and climbing their sylvan slopes. 'I love the way they contain you, and then open up every now and then. And then they take you back into the shadows and the dappled light.' As always, he thinks of how he can translate the experience into architecture: 'I had an idea for land berms that would get you up above tree lines. Maybe that is what I am thinking of for the new building for the transit authority.'

Angkor, Cambodia (2000), by Andrew Bromberg. Shelter: cool stone passages resisting the surrounding tropical jungle.

Climbing steps carved into the hillside, through a small gate, visitors arrive at a bridge that crosses a steep, forested canyon. The view is exhilarating, as if you are floating on the treetops. Signs of Singapore's dense population peeking above the trees in the distance prompts Bromberg to recall his childhood: 'One thing I always imagine is finding the tallest tree and climbing up. It just draws me, getting up there and finally seeing where you are. I guess it came from the book *The Hobbit*, the passage where [Bilbo] escaped by going up in the trees. And then he could finally see everything, and everything was all right after that. That's what I would want to do.' Today Bromberg constantly takes pictures and makes sketches, noting strange arrangements of branches that might be useful for his buildings.

Although Singapore had a formative influence on Bromberg's early Asian years ('it was the first city in Asia I visited,' he remembers; 'I had no money and I just walked and walked through these dense streets'), his experience with the city today is different: 'I still love wandering past the shophouses and downtown, but I spend most of my time in meetings and in cars. I have to be reminded of the qualities of what makes this such an amazing city. But I also now have a more vertical orientation, I guess. I always loved skyscrapers, but looking down from them, not up. That was my first memory of tall buildings, going with my father to his offices and looking down from there at Denver. I want to design to create that feeling, looking down and around.'

'I always loved skyscrapers, but looking down from them, not up. I want to design to create that feeling'

The sense of the separation – between nature and the city, and between the place of refuge and otherness, and the more familiar, if sometimes alienating, environment of stores, office buildings, restaurants and apartment blocks – seems proper to this architect. However much he talks about wanting to create buildings covered with nature and exploring nature for inspiration, he remains an architect for whom nature is something to be explored and exploited, while architecture presents a refined version of whatever Eden he finds.

'Shelter: a basic need to be protected from our environment – but not by being sterilized from the freedom of nature, air, smells and sounds; human sustainability'

The Star

Singapore
Status: Built (2012)
GFA: 62,000 m² (667,000 ft²)
Site Area: 19,200 m² (206,700 ft²)
Building Height: 75 m (246 ft)

The design for the Star Performing Arts Centre does not present one singular expression to describe the project; instead it celebrates the rich and numerous activities inside with a multi-faceted permeable and dynamic design, blurring the boundaries between the public and private realms and between the retail and cultural components. These transitions are soft and flowing, encouraging discovery and resulting in a highly public, energetic attraction for the city.

Developing an architectural language to express both commercial and civic components of the project was paramount. The design allows for the south elevation to be completely opened up, presenting the inner workings of the facility as a section visible from and to the landscaped areas. The mass of the upper cultural component is faceted, intersecting glass fissures through the titanium cladding. These features help to reduce the visual impact of the overall volume, playing with a composition of positive and negative readings of the theatre in balance with the use of solid and void in the retail component.

The building is intended to be an organic object which is open to public discovery. One can crawl under, move through, transverse and climb onto the structure through a series of ramps, escalators, terraces and public gardens. All circulation, movement and internal forms are soft and sinuous through the flow of activities, presenting a calming interior that contrasts with the strongly urban faceted exterior.

The cultural and retail components are bound together with the 40-m (130-ft) high volume of the 'Grand Foyer'. The importance of these two components to each other is celebrated by blurring the divisions between them while maintaining functionality.

The design is highly sustainable, making use of natural cooling to minimize air-conditioned spaces. Incorporating openings in all four elevations encourages air movement through the volume; the result is an enjoyable year-round shaded environment with a cooling breeze allowing one to pass through or dwell within.

The Grand Foyer, looking east

130

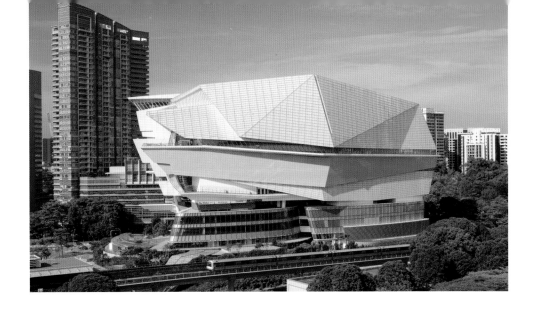

Auditorium above retail space, looking south

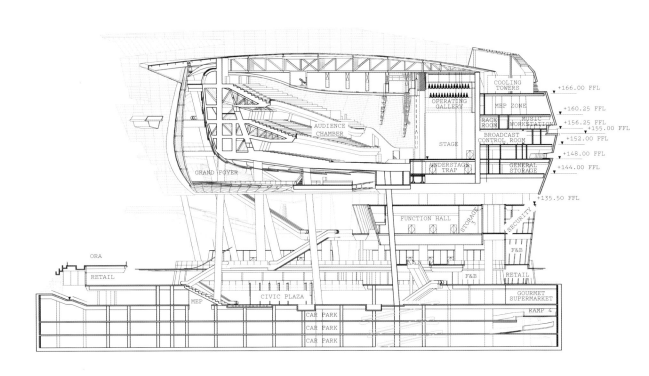

Longitudinal section

Competition concept sketch by Andrew Bromberg

Aerial view, looking east
OVERLEAF View looking west

Foyers, eastern façade

400-m (1,300-ft) public loop, 40 m (130 ft) above
the ground

Bridge level, looking down to civic plaza

Level three Grand Foyer escalator connection
to the performing arts centre

138

The Star Vista, Grand Foyer

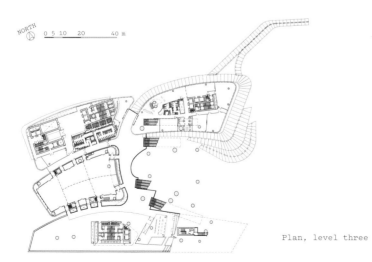

NORTH   0 5 10   20   40 m

Plan, level three

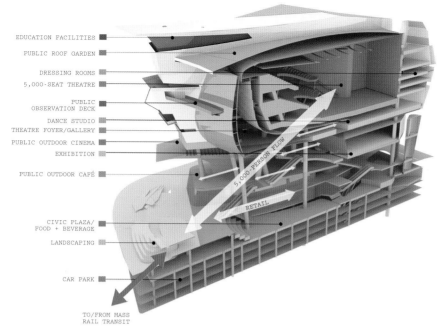

EDUCATION FACILITIES

PUBLIC ROOF GARDEN

DRESSING ROOMS
5,000-SEAT THEATRE

PUBLIC
OBSERVATION DECK

DANCE STUDIO
THEATRE FOYER/GALLERY
PUBLIC OUTDOOR CINEMA
EXHIBITION

PUBLIC OUTDOOR CAFÉ

CIVIC PLAZA/
FOOD + BEVERAGE

LANDSCAPING

CAR PARK

TO/FROM MASS
RAIL TRANSIT

5,000-PERSON FLOW

RETAIL

Flow diagram between the retail spaces
and auditorium

Level five, outer lobby

Auditorium, the 5,000-seat performing arts centre

Sandcrawler

Singapore
Status: Built (2013)
GFA: 21,468 m² (231,080 ft²)
Site Area: 61,816 m² (665,382 ft²)
Building Height: 58 m (190 ft²)

Sandcrawler is both a regional headquarters for a major entertainment company, and a revenue-generating office building. Combining this with a strong civic intent within the One North masterplan, the design for this project not only enjoys this ambiguity but also seeks a resolution which celebrates the diversity. The masterplanning guidelines are highly defined, dictating envelope height and setbacks. What is unusual about the controls is that they stipulate not only a certain height but a specific sloping topography. The guidelines also regulate the minimum amount of mass on the enclosure. The design approaches these guidelines deliberately to fulfil the viability requirements but with a strong civic quality as a statement for the local headquarters. The result is that the building floats up to 13 m (43 ft) above the ground below. The open space is landscaped in a natural, overgrown manner. It has been proposed that the pedestrian space might provide a public connection to the MRT subway.

The façade addresses different audiences and contexts. The external metallic glass skin provides good solar protection and privacy on the more exposed faces as well as presenting an aerodynamic appearance. On the lower edges the skin is cut away and uses a low-iron clear glass. This glass is also used in the end faces of the wings, and into the courtyard elevations as well as wrapping under the vessel's soffit. The client requested a state-of-the-art 100-seat cinema. This facility relates directly to the end-user tenant of the entertainment company. The facility needed a double-height zone and was placed on the upper levels of the lower, end-user zone and immediately below the leased tenant spaces. Conferencing facilities, a gallery and pre-function facilities as well as an external patio were also located in the same zone.

Public green, civic courtyard

View of the 'prow' from the northeast

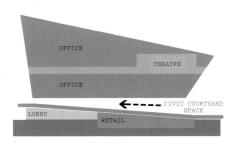

Sectional diagram

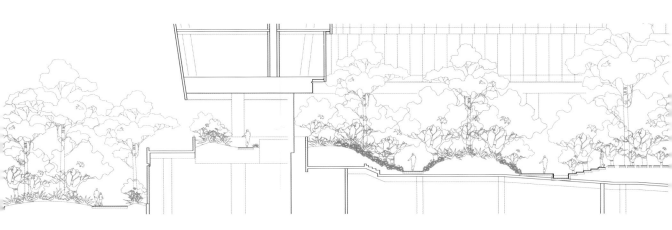

Landscape section, civic courtyard

View from the northwest

View from the north

100-seat high-performance screening theatre

Main lobby below the civic courtyard

146

Staff pantry, looking into the civic green

Pre-function area for the theatre

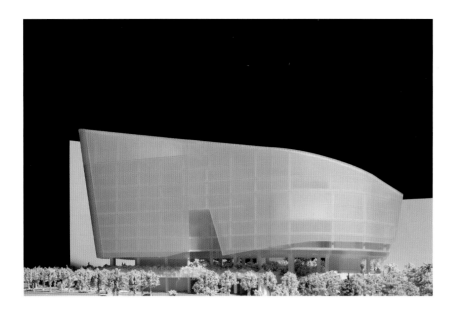

Model of south elevation

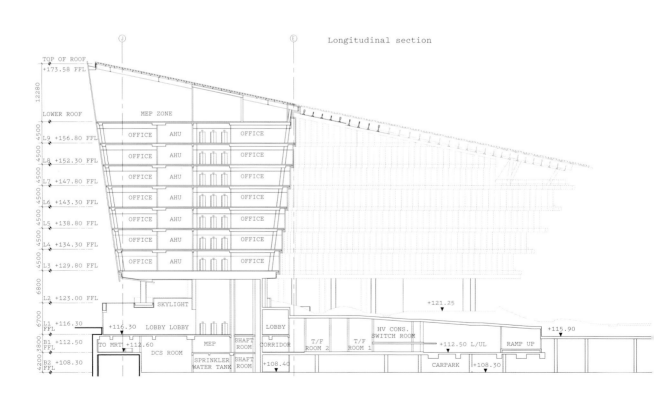

Longitudinal section

TOP OF ROOF
+173.58 FFL

12280

LOWER ROOF

4500

MEP ZONE

L9 +156.80 FFL | OFFICE | AHU | OFFICE
4500
L8 +152.30 FFL | OFFICE | AHU | OFFICE
4500
L7 +147.80 FFL | OFFICE | AHU | OFFICE
4500
L6 +143.30 FFL | OFFICE | AHU | OFFICE
4500
L5 +138.80 FFL | OFFICE | AHU | OFFICE
4500
L4 +134.30 FFL | OFFICE | AHU | OFFICE
4500
L3 +129.80 FFL | OFFICE | AHU | OFFICE

6800

L2 +123.00 FFL

SKYLIGHT

6700

L1 +116.30 FFL

+116.30   LOBBY LOBBY

+121.25

LOBBY

B1 +112.50 FFL
3800
TO MRT +112.60   DCS ROOM   MEP   SHAFT ROOM   CORRIDOR   T/F ROOM 2   T/F ROOM 1   HV CONS. SWITCH ROOM   +112.50 L/UL   RAMP UP
+115.90

B2 +108.30 FFL
4200
SPRINKLER WATER TANK   SHAFT ROOM   +108.40   CARPARK   +108.30

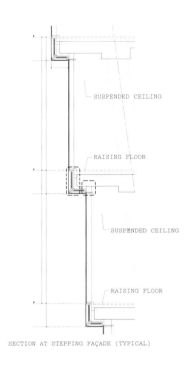

SUSPENDED CEILING

RAISING FLOOR

SUSPENDED CEILING

RAISING FLOOR

SECTION AT STEPPING FAÇADE (TYPICAL)

Inside courtyard,
wall-section details

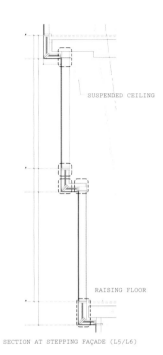

SUSPENDED CEILING

RAISING FLOOR

SECTION AT STEPPING FAÇADE (L5/L6)

Model, looking at the 'prow'

Landscape plan

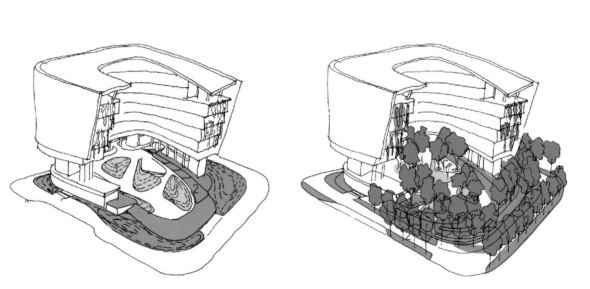

Landscape concept diagrams

Looking east into the horseshoe courtyard

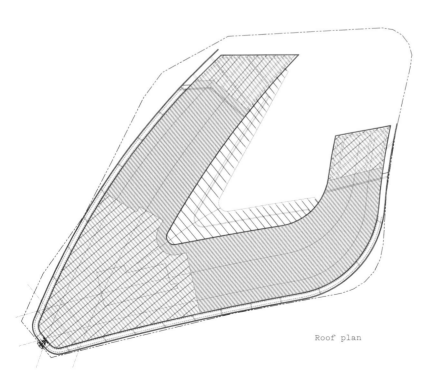

Roof plan

Kortrijk Blekerij

Kortrijk, Belgium
Status: Schematic Design
GFA: 30,000 m² (322,917 ft²)
Site Area: 30,717 m² (330,635 ft²)
Building Height: 52 m (171 ft)

Kortrijk Blekerij is a residential-focused, mixed-use project in Kortrijk, Belgium. Historically the site was an old textile factory, which was the industry that had previously defined the city. Today, the town is actively pursuing a more lifestyle-oriented approach to its environment through a range of civic-minded developments. These include an extensive network of walking/ biking trails, which tie all of the urban open spaces together. The design for Kortrijk Blekerij strives to 'weave' – both figuratively and literally – together the modern city's civic space ambitions and its rich history in textiles.

The low-rise commercial elements were placed off the busy road to the east, as well as wrapping around to the north, along with the main vehicular entries and a zone of assisted living. Two more layers of low-rise townhouses splay inward from the northeast corner. This focuses the development on to a quiet, protected green square opening on to the river to the south. The square becomes a node along the network of trails which connect the river edge to the north of the city along a greenbelt placed on the western edge of the site. This public square is supported by retail, café and restaurant developments.

Loosely defining the square to the south are two 50-m (165-ft) high residential towers, with units commanding views up and down the river and anchoring the development.
The small floor-plate towers still provide a dense concentration that allows for the open space to exist as well as street walls tying into the urban fabric of the adjacent context. They explore a 'woven' formality, and are placed close to the previous 'stacks' of the factory.

Rendering, aerial view over Burgemeester Lambrechtlaan bridge

Concept, Kortrijk textile
industry

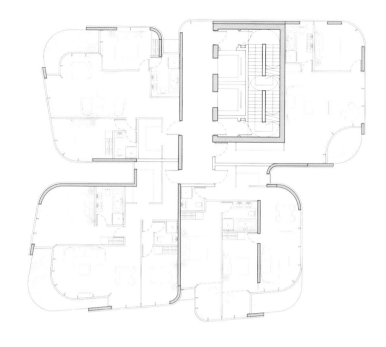

Typical floor unit layout plan

Rendering, looking north

Rendering, aerial view, looking north

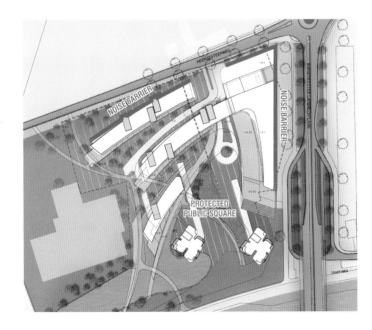

Site plan

Huafa Arts Center

Zhuhai, China
Status: Concept
GFA: 20,000 m² (215,000 ft²)
Site Area: 19,200 m² (206,700 ft²)
Building Height: 71 m (233 ft)

The Huafa Arts Center, located between the Gongbei border crossing station and the sea, is positioned in what may be the most pivotal site in the city of Zhuhai. The immigration facilities are the busiest in the world, as the major connection between mainland China and Macau. Reinforcing the importance of the HAC's location is its role as a conclusion to the 28-km (17-mile) seaside promenade of Lover's Road, which ends abruptly at the Macau border immediately after the site. The civic value of this project is understood by the city, with the previous proposal being for a municipal park before it was considered for a cultural facility.

An uncompromising solution was sought that combines the civic aspirations of both park and museum while at the same time providing a significant and celebrated resolution to Lover's Road. The ground plane was tilted diagonally, rising from the northeast corner at Lover's Road to the southwest corner towards the border facilities and Macau. This provides two edges and a park facing out on to the sunrise over the sea and back towards Zhuhai, while also providing more contextual 'urban' edges to the border crossings.

The volume beneath this plane is optimized to take advantage of the larger surface components of the museum, including a bookstore and café, conferencing facilities, storage, administration and studios, as well as the large exhibition space of the museum itself.

To signify the importance of the site as a terminus to Lover's Road and the edge of Zhuhai, the project itself needed to be a prominent physical marker. Historically, stacked stones have been used all over the world to indicate a place of significance. They occur at the top of Mount Everest, for example. In China they are often called 'lovers' rocks' – an appropriate statement to end Lover's Road!

These stacked 'stones', rising 71 m (233 ft) from the street, are inhabited by the remaining exhibition spaces, an art education centre and public facilities on top. This affords the public spaces and circulation areas amazing views out to the sea and the city of Zhuhai, while at the same time forming a marker which designates the transition between the two border cities – visible from Lover's Road, from Macau and from the sea – both by boat and, in the near future, from the new Hong Kong/Zhuhai/Macau bridge.

Competition model, looking west

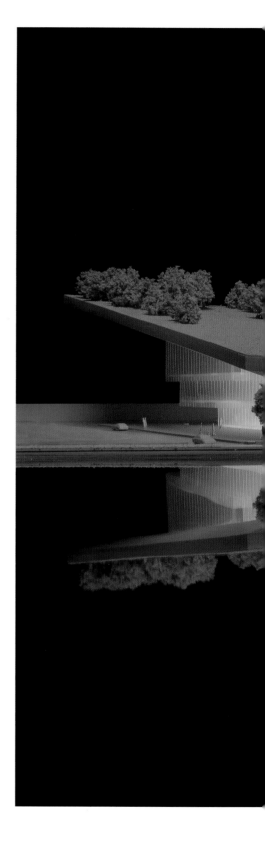

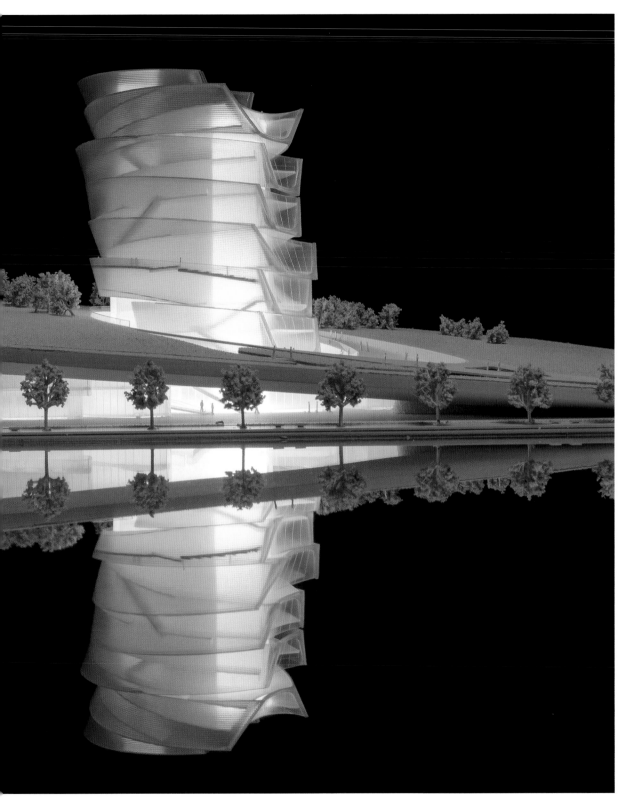

Vertical circulation system diagrams

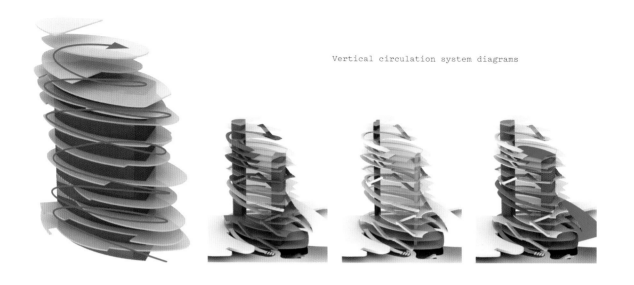

Rendering, looking west

Rendering, 'tilted green', looking south to Macau

Museum lobby below the 'tilted green'

Rendering, a typical gallery

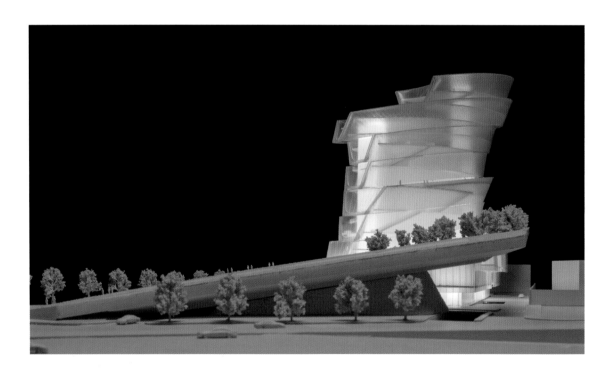

Model, southwest corner

Rendering, stack galleries at night

Abdul Latif Jameel's Corporate Headquarters

Jeddah, Saudi Arabia
Status: Planning
GFA: 46,900 m² (504,800 ft²)
Site Area: 6,786 m² (73,044 ft²)
Building Height: 102.6 m (336.6 ft)

The project is located within a prime 21-hectare (52-acre) site north of Al-Balad, the historic part of Jeddah, close to the airport. It is connected to Prince Majid Road, one of the main north–south roads across the city. The site is undergoing new masterplanning, part of which includes Abdul Latif Jameel's Corporate Headquarters building.

ALJ's Corporate Headquarters will anchor the northwest corner of the masterplan. The facility is located at the intersection of a secondary road and the main artery connecting Jeddah's airport to the old town and the modern city of Jeddah. The two faces adjacent to the roads are used as a buffer for the 'living' spaces of the complex. Inspired by the traditional buildings of Jeddah, these 'protective' plaster faces are relatively solid in appearance, and limit the penetration of the harsh western light into the building as well as mitigating the noise from the busy streets.

These faces evolved to become independent 'L-bar' volumes, which contain all support functions including service cores, conference facilities, canteens, gym, prayer rooms and toilets. This allows adjacent offices, separated by an atrium, to achieve maximum efficiency through open planning with ultimate flexibility of space. In contrast to the L-bars facing the streets, the office space is contained in a 'soft, flowing, highly transparent skin', reflecting the ethos of the company.

Office floors are stacked in clusters of three, with intermediate interaction-zone floors where users can have more casual meetings or breaks within lounge spaces, provided to create a sense of community. On the podium roof there is a communal garden, and a running track meanders in and out of various spaces within the development.

Rendering, looking north

162

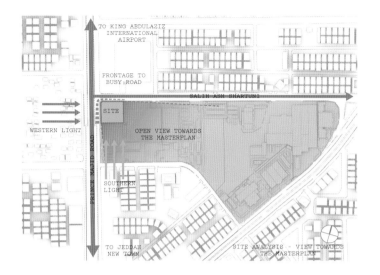

Overall masterplan

Inside the diagram:

TO KING ABDULAZIZ
INTERNATIONAL
AIRPORT

FRONTAGE TO
BUSY ROAD

SALIH ASH SHARTUNI

WESTERN LIGHT

PRINCE MAJID ROAD

SITE

OPEN VIEW TOWARDS
THE MASTERPLAN

SOUTHERN
LIGHT

TO JEDDAH
NEW TOWN

SITE ANALYSIS - VIEW TOWARDS
THE MASTERPLAN

North-south highway connection, the airport
to the old town

East-west section through atrium

ROOF FLOOR
102.6 m

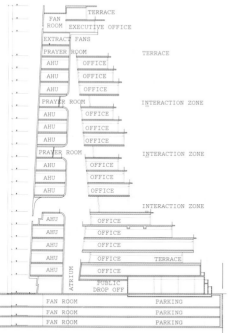

West façade from highway

North façade at night

Low-level U-shaped office plan

Renderings inside the 'tempered' atrium
OVERLEAF Rendering, plaza view looking north

166

DUBAI: BUILDING BETWEEN THE TWO SUNS

The Taj Mahal, Agra, India (1995), by Andrew Bromberg. Objects:
rushing to experience the volume of the dome, only to discover it
is not visible.

'You are suffering from the effects of two suns,' explained Michael Fowler, one of Andrew Bromberg's associates, during a visit to Dubai in the middle of summer. 'First there is the heat of the sun overhead, and there is very little escape from that anywhere outside. Then there is the reflection of that sun, originally on the desert, but now on all the concrete and asphalt that makes up the new landscape of Dubai. It is not the sun that kills you, it is the double sun.' Bromberg explains that in most desert cities, 'You go outside and it's still hot at 2 a.m., but if you go into the desert at 2 a.m. it's cold. Here you have all this paving that holds all the ambient heat. So why do they do that? Why do they have all this paving here?'

The Taj Mahal, Agra, India (1995), by Andrew Bromberg. Objects: perfect symmetry, with the mosque to the west (left of image) and the false mosque to the east.

It was a question that kept arising in Dubai, an 'instant city' that grew from a pearl-fishing and trading post of around 50,000 inhabitants in 1950 to a city of 2.5 million and one of the world's great commerce, finance and shipping centres today. Dubai is where Bromberg first made his mark as an independent designer, in a place where the natural and the human-made have both achieved a level of abstraction - alien to the human body and resisting a sense of culture and community. And now Bromberg has a new project here; then again there is always something new to see in Dubai, which works hard to produce ever larger and ever stranger urban scenes.

The site for the architect's new building is a structure meant to house a hotel and service apartments. The site is located across from a shopping centre in what the developers call 'Downtown Dubai'. The area has become the de facto core of what developed as a linear city, moving from the mouth of Dubai

Creek, where the original settlement was located, north towards
the source of most of the United Arab Emirates' wealth, the oil
fields of Abu Dhabi. Downtown focuses on what is, at least
for now, the tallest building in the world, the Burj Khalifa.
It is a structure that, at a height of almost 200 floors,
is impossible to comprehend. It makes all the buildings around
it look minuscule, until you realize that many of them are
fifty to seventy storeys tall. The Burj stands opposite
a luxury shopping mall, on the shores of an artificial lake
lined with hotels and residential developments that reach back
past courtyards and plazas to a broad boulevard that circles
the inner development. Office, residential and hotel towers
radiate out from there, before fading into a no-man's-land of
highways and empty plots next to adjacent developments.

'The Burj is a loss leader,' Bromberg suggests. 'It makes
little sense by itself, but it sells everything else. They can
charge ten times more rent for anything that faces the tower.'
His own first contribution to Downtown, the twin-towered
Boulevard Plaza, serves as a gateway to the whole development.
'It was difficult: the Burj Khalifa is their pride and joy,
but you want to do something that has some power and holds its own, that defines the site in its own way. So, I worked to give these two buildings, which are quite a bit smaller, a presence. They shape your sense of orientation as you move around the confusing circle of Downtown, because of the duality

Outside Puno, Peru (1999), by Andrew Bromberg. Objects:
the Aymara's Sillustani chullpas funeral markers.

between the two, the way they play off each other. We also got
very lucky with how the glass we used for the skins works with
the towers' curves. Because of that, the buildings have a much
more shimmering quality than everything around them. There is

a haziness here because of all the dust blowing in from the desert, and these buildings seem to repel that.' Indeed, the towers do stand out from the other structures around them, orienting the visitor arriving from the main north-south axis of Sheikh Zayed Road.

Within the development, the Burj seems ever present, but doesn't help locate you in the abstract landscape because its architecture is so slick. 'The Burj Khalifa may be the anchor piece,' Bromberg explains, 'but you still don't recognize the different sides. You can be on any side and you're not going to recognize any one side. Then you're just walking or driving around in a circle, without any sense of orientation. Outside this circle you have endless buildings. If you know the area, you can identify a few, or an architect can pick out ones designed by Norman Foster or Zaha Hadid. But the majority of the people quickly get lost. I'd like to think that, by having

'I think all of this was designed for the nighttime, for the lighting effects and the spectacle they put on. There's no life during the day, no shade'

two different towers that are not twin towers and that have a relationship to each other that in turn changes as you move around them, it might help create some orientation.'

Bromberg makes another interesting point related to the challenges of the development. 'I think all of this was designed for the nighttime, for the lighting effects and the spectacle they put on then when they light up the Burj Khalifa and everybody comes out and promenades around the lake. It seems to have no value right now. There's no life during the day, no shade.'

One of the side streets off the main development leads into a residential development. 'Here,' Bromberg says, pointing out the contrast, 'the street is inviting, there's a scale to it, there's not a lot of traffic. You feel like you're in a residential environment, which is quite different than the surrounding streets - there are birds everywhere! There are local people, coming out doing their daily errands and rituals, local retail, a pharmacy, a salon-spa, a grocery around the corner. I'm not saying that this is a prime example of urbanity, but this feels strangely good to me.' But perhaps the question of whether this makes up part of a real city remains. Bromberg replies: 'We're talking about isolated compounds. That area next to us looks very inviting, for example, but you can't get there and you're not allowed to be there. There should be a public promenade.'

'Dubai in itself is an oasis to the whole Gulf region. Artificial or not, it is the place that all the Saudis and Kuwaitis escape to from their own environments'

This turns out to be a double conundrum in Dubai: public space everywhere is just leftover and unshaded, while interiors and private areas are exclusive utopias disconnected from everything else. The human-made environments mimic the overall position of Dubai as an artificial oasis at the edge of the Saharan desert. It is not just a question of the addition – at great cost – of greenery and water that enabled the city to grow, but of the social and economic reasons for that growth. Dubai set itself up as the 'free zone' on the Arabian Peninsula, a place to play and to earn money with few of the restrictions that many found so stifling in its neighbours. Dubai, in other words, is a social as well as a physical oasis, though one that is as limited in its freedoms as in its shade. Only the very wealthy expatriots, cocooned in their shopping malls, hotels, offices or apartments, can, for as long as the government allows them (they can never become citizens), enjoy a respite from the barren social and physical climate all around the city-state. As Bromberg says: 'Dubai in itself is an oasis to the whole Gulf region. Artificial or not, it is the place that all the Saudis and Kuwaitis escape to from their own environments.'

As a result, architects in Dubai can push their fantasies much further than in other locations, and Bromberg has been lucky to have received so many commissions here. However,

his experience also highlights the constraints in place.
The 172-m (564-ft) high twins were actually meant to be six
storeys higher, which would have improved their proportions,
as he admits himself, but the client wanted a more efficient
building. At the Promenade, a residential tower and office block
sitting on top of a large parking plinth he designed in another
semicircular development, Business Bay, the public plaza that
was meant to be a place
of gathering in the
tall structures' shade
remains forlorn and
unfinished. The client
did not want to spend
the money on space
that would not bring
any income. Meanwhile
one of Bromberg's
residential projects
stopped midway after
the global financial
crisis of 2008, and
another was subsequently
finished in a rather
haphazard manner.
Freedom, in other
words, is constrained
by financial concerns.
The Dubai developers see
strong forms as ways to
advertise their wares
and compete with each
other, but they must
also follow a financial
logic.

Yangon, Myanmar (2000), by Andrew Bromberg. Objects:
the golden Shwedagon Pagoda, the oldest Buddhist stupa
in the world.

What makes it
difficult for an
architect and a foreign
observer to understand
is that the economic logic is not always apparent. On a weekday,
for example, the three- and four-storey walkways in the shopping
mall opposite the Burj Khalifa are largely empty. However,

Bagan, Myanmar (1999), by Andrew Bromberg. Objects: 2,000
ancient stone monuments dotting the landscape as far as the
eye can see.

Dubai's shopping and eating scene is apparently tied to an
enduring desert culture that means people come out only in
the evenings, even if in the city, the climate is not much
cooler then.

Even stranger, seemingly, is the ability of such towers
as the Burj Khalifa to survive purely as a form of advertisement
for the other real estate in Downtown, but apparently it
works well enough that a competing developer is planning a
spire almost twice as high that will have no function other
than as an observation platform and monument. 'I can't figure it
out,' Bromberg laments. 'I designed a perfectly good tower for
that site, but that time I guess they didn't want logic. But when
I designed an opera house for Dubai Creek that might have looked
a little crazy, but was a perfect response to the site, the
programme and how the client had described what they were looking
for, they thought it was too far out.'

There is also the effect of the landscape that renders it difficult to make a visually attractive and place-sensitive design in Dubai. Here the most brightly coloured buildings with the tightest glass skins around them can look dull, drab and muffled against a hazy sky. It tends to be a rather monochrome place, and the light is not very bright. The sand blows around and colours the light, engulfing the place in a homogeneous haze, making an abstract, blank environment. This means that the desert, which the government and the developers worked so hard to keep at bay in Dubai, still has a pervasive quality, lending an essence of sand to the whole city. It creates an essential lack of differentiation that is proper to the desert, but no matter how hard architects here work to make buildings catch your eye, and no matter how high they build their towers, the sameness takes over.

It is, of course, not only the sand that dominates. There is also a lack of clear natural landmarks, as well as any urban masterplanning that could provide differentiation, so that the city is not layered and does not reveal itself. This character serves landmarks such as the Burj Khalifa well, but it does not help to provide more general orientation. Dubai has abandoned the Creek, the interruption in the sandy coastline where it began, and has turned its back on the ocean. Where it does reach out into the water, as in the Palm developments and the World Islands, it does so with forms that are again repetitive - fronds of imaginary palm trees in the former, groups of blobs meant to resemble continents in the latter - and that only make sense when you fly in and out of its airport.

Yangon, Myanmar (1999), by Andrew Bromberg. Objects: Shwedagon Pagoda, surrounded by Buddhist shrines.

Inside the city's buildings, air-conditioning and design banish the sameness, at least for a moment. Then you realize you could be anywhere: the stores in the shopping malls are all the same, the office and hotel lobbies look the same, and even the restaurants, despite their Arab themes, could be in Singapore or London. It is not just that the brands are universal - so too are the bits and pieces out of which everything is built. You find the same granite paving, marble walls, cheaper white walls in between, mass-produced fittings and glass assemblies out of which we make buildings anywhere.

Paradoxically, these are the elements that make Dubai part of a wider culture, helping to elevate it from the landscape in which it sits. It sums up the most efficient construction and urban development processes, the ability of buildings to compete in height and design, the standardization of taste, design and function, and all the other aspects of the early 21st-century city that let urban nomads live anywhere. Unencumbered by mountains or by history, Dubai has been able to do it bigger, taller and faster than any other city since the mid-20th century. What it has not yet figured out, for all its freedom and despite the best efforts by architects such as Bromberg, is how to do it better.

'I don't mind the flatness, but there are no mountains. You need mountains. When I was growing up in Colorado and you looked down from the Rockies, even the plains reaching out to Nebraska looked beautiful'

It did not start that way. With Bromberg and Fowler, I visited the area around the old fort, Dubai's symbolic core. It was cooler here, both because of breezes coming off the water, and because the relatively low buildings, filled with small shops and apartments, rose up on narrow streets offering plenty of shade. We drank tea in a rebuilt courtyard house, its fake stucco walls and imported

tile providing a theme-park version of the original, but its
spaces were pleasant to occupy. 'Why can't they build things
with this grain, with this quality of space?' Bromberg asked.
'Some developers are thinking about it,' Fowler answered, 'but
nobody has figured out how to make enough money doing it.'

If you move out of the Creek, from an area of buildings and
boats to the more common clumps of high-rise towers, apartment
blocks and
hermetically
sealed shopping
malls, you arrive
at the edge of
the built-up
area, at real
desert, and a vast
flat landscape.
'I don't mind
the flatness,'
Bromberg says,
'but there are
no mountains. You
need mountains.
When I was growing
up in Colorado
and you looked
down from the

Angkor, Cambodia (1999), by Andrew Bromberg. Objects:
the ever-watching faces of Angkor Thom.

Rockies, even the plains reaching out to Nebraska looked
beautiful, and the same when you were in those fields looking
towards the ridges to the west.

'Dubai is essentially a linear succession of isolated
blocks,' Bromberg explains. 'The royal family owns the whole
place. They give out blocks of desert to develop, one at a time.
Sometimes they decided what the theme is going to be, like when
they created an area that was supposed to be a Media City.
What it really means is that each area is disconnected from the
next. There is absolutely no incentive for anybody to connect
to their neighbour, and because nobody walks here, there is
no pressure from the public to create that kind of connective
tissue. Plus, when they have sold their plots, they are done,
why spend money keeping things up? They're done and on to the
next project.'

The government does provide plentiful roads, of course, and has also built other infrastructure, including what will soon be the largest and busiest airport in the world, a large container port and a massive power plant. It has also constructed a rudimentary mass transit system, which mainly functions to ferry the poorly paid workers who usually live in temporary shelters on undeveloped land to the places where they work and back again. The core of all that work is, in fact, not an oasis-like hub – it is the spine of Sheikh Zayed Road.

'When I first came to Dubai,' Bromberg reminisces, 'the city was much more clear. You could see all the main buildings going north or south, and the city had a certain clarity to it. It was a truly linear city, not like an American city, where there is a centre of density and then it quiets down moving towards the outskirts. Here, the road was totally edged with buildings on either side. If you go to the back of these buildings, you will still see that it's all sand and utilitarian parking structures. Which always implied to me that there was never an intention for that edge to grow. It would just be duplicated behind by a parallel boulevard, or somebody would build another centre further inland and then would feed on to Sheikh Zayed.' It is similar to the way Las Vegas grew around the Strip, for example – perhaps it has something to do with travelling through the desert, as in all those old Western movies; you have the main path going in and there are all these buildings that look substantial on either side of you. Then you go around the back and realize that all the façades are propped up to make the buildings look a lot taller. The one advantage of the row of developments, you might argue, is that it can create an urban rhythm that can subsume even the strangest or most mediocre building by creating a pattern. 'That is true,' Bromberg says, 'but that only works as you are driving by at high speed on this elevated road. At the ground, everything separates again, so it all falls apart.'

There are alternative models. In nearby Abu Dhabi, the model for a more sustainable development stands unfinished. Called Masdar City, it was designed by the British architect Norman Foster. It was meant to be a city of 50,000 inhabitants that would be 'net zero', meaning it would only use energy it generated through solar panels, wind turbines and recycling. You were meant to leave your car at the city's edge and travel around

Florence, Italy (1993), by Andrew Bromberg. Objects:
Brunelleschi's Duomo is more than an icon; it is the
true symbol of the city.

Chandigarh, India (1995), by Andrew Bromberg.
Objects: Le Corbusier's Palace of Assembly, oculus over
the main hall.

in automated pods. However, only a tiny portion was actually
constructed and today it sits by itself in a construction site
that appears to be a burial ground of bold ideas.

We wandered through a maze of small streets, past a few
stores and restaurants. 'This works in the sense that we are
in shade,' commented Bromberg, 'but you get lost because it is
a kit of parts. There is no logic to their orientation, either
in how you move through here or where the sun comes from. I
would go underground,' he said, 'outside of Djerba in Tunisia,
all the indigenous dwellings are underground. It's where George
Lucas went for Luke Skywalker's house, which is actually a real
home. That's how they've been living for thousands of years.
Glass towers seem like the opposite thing you should do in
this environment.' Bromberg has tried, designing a resort as

one of the desert oases that was meant to be carved into the ground, mimicking the pattern of seasonal wadis or streambeds. 'Everything is geared to making saleable blocks and towers.'

Bromberg has designed three towers at an area of the northern side of Sheikh Zayed Road, called Dubai Marina. Here, it is possible to walk along the water's edge in one continuous line, even if the path goes around the towers, making what at first appears a short distance lengthen into miles of switchbacks. 'Even here, there is no shade or planting, nothing to make this a pleasant place to be,' Bromberg observes. The developers sold their units and moved on, while the owners of the apartments seem to make little use of the few amenities on offer.

'Glass towers seem like the opposite thing you should do in this environment'

The most elegant of the structures Bromberg designed here, Ocean Heights, is eighty-two storeys tall. It curves to one side, maximizing the views from the most expensive apartments at the top. Along the way, the back of the building, which emphasizes the horizontal stack of floors, gives way to a sweeping sail in blue-green glass. A few fins, which are actually balconies, stitch the two together. Compared with the squat towers all around it, Ocean Heights soars. Bromberg is satisfied with the result, but says he wanted more balconies. 'It is like calling for better space to walk,' he explains. 'They say that nobody uses those outdoor spaces.'

Pentominium, a so-called 'super-tall' building of 122 storeys, was supposed to have been, at 518 m (1,699 ft), the tallest residential structure in the world. However, construction was halted in 2009 after one of the deepest excavations ever, and the first twenty-three floors built. The building would have been a twisting and curving needle whose skins would have unravelled as the structure rose to a thin turret. Bromberg explained what happened: 'The developers would pre-sell units, take the money, and invest it in the next building, assuming they would keep selling to finish the first building. When the market dried up and everybody started leaving town, they had no money left to finish buildings. It is coming back, but things are still not back to where they were. Part of the problem with Dubai is that all these developments happened overnight; they never actually spotted places to improve things. They could have done phases for example, but they didn't. Now we will have to wait and see.'

It is possible to take the view that his Dubai towers might be anywhere. 'Once you start doing these three-, four- and five-hundred metre towers,' he points out, 'you are basically only focusing on horizon. You've divorced yourself from the streetscape. When I grew up I was fascinated by skyscrapers; like every architect, I wanted to create objects. But somehow, when I was over here, it became formalistic in a way that I wouldn't use as a compliment. It was just shape-making, not place-making. I got to a point where making towers was becoming slightly dissatisfying, and I didn't want to be typecast as a tower architect. I would like to believe that I can do a tower that becomes more part of a pattern and can contribute, however romantic that sounds, to the life of the city. I want to improve the urban fabric more than create silhouettes in the landscape.'

Who actually lives in these towers? Bromberg had an answer: 'I have friends who live around here, and they love it. It is safe, their kids can go to decent schools, there is a lot of shopping and entertainment. They don't seem to mind that there is little culture or community.' Could Dubai become a new version of Miami, along with a new version of an American 'edge city' development of offices, shopping, and apartments along a highway? 'It could, but, again, there is no life here, no great beaches like you have there, no Coconut Grove,' Bromberg answered. Could that happen with time? 'Maybe.'

'I still like working here, despite everything,' Bromberg says. 'Sure, Dubai could have embraced the natural landscape more, celebrated it even. But instead they wanted to try to create a recognizable city. Once you create that recognizable city you're kind of turning your back on the landscape. I lived in Arizona for a year. I was on camels in India with just one little five-year-old kid taking me around. I went to the gateway of the Sahara in Tunisia one year. I've always had an amazing fascination with deserts. Dubai never gave me an opportunity to really address the desert because I had projects that were landlocked on little sites. But I keep hoping.'

'Objects: shaped and moulded by environmental, functional and experiential forces that have defined and are defining space and place'

Da Wang Jing Mixed-use Development

Beijing, China
Status: Built (2016)
GFA: 571,878 m² (6,155,644 ft²)
Site Area: 305,510 m² (3,288,482 ft²)
Building Height: 220 m (722 ft)

Da Wang Jing Mixed-use Development is located in the Dawangjing area of Cuigezhuang township in the Chaoyang district of Beijing, and is bounded on the northeast by East Fifth Ring Road, on the south by Dawangjing Street, on the northwest by a new Wangjing artery and on the southwest by Wangjing No. 2 Road.

The project site consists of three individual parcels with a variety of properties proposed, including four high-rise office towers, a high-rise apartment building and a multi-functional commercial and convention complex. Apart from towers, podiums offer private and corporate clubhouses, retail, restaurants and bars, banks and entertainment. Office towers are designed as Grade A office spaces and corporate headquarters.

The development is surrounded by residential and commercial plot typologies, with Dawangjing Park and planned green spaces on the southern edge. The design simulates the concept of an oasis, aiming to accentuate its relationship to the surrounding greenery, and guaranteeing maximum permeability to facilitate public access. The design of the development is unique, with its flowing, organic character encouraging its users to explore the spaces within while echoing its exclusive commercial auxiliary facilities and high-end apartments. The iconic building masses can be perceived as a complex of integrity: a respectable image appropriate for a corporate headquarters intended as a dominant commercial landmark in the Dawangjing area, as well as Beijing City as a whole.

Street view, looking north

View looking up between the towers

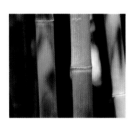

Bamboo concept image

View looking southwest

View looking north

Interior view, tower lobby

OPPOSITE Ground view,
looking northwest

DAMAC Heights

Dubai, United Arab Emirates
Status: Built (2017)
GFA: 114,000 m² (1,228,000 ft²)
Site Area: 3,240 m² (34,875 ft²)
Building Height: 335 m (1,099 ft)

DAMAC Heights, being located in the heart of Dubai Marina, United Arab Emirates, where it is surrounded by many architectural objects, sought a singular powerful gesture to give it the presence to rise above its neighbours. As two blades bending together 335 m (1,099 ft) above the ground, the project reduces in area as it sharpens into the sky. The project is located along with its 'sister' project, Ocean Heights. DAMAC Heights, with 105 floors, is one of the tallest towers in the area. However, unlike its predecessor, the requirements for modularized units up to the sixtieth floor forced a different approach, with the challenge being to maintain the spirit of its 'sculptural' sister.

The first two-thirds of the residential tower are designed to be flexible, allowing for three possible uses: residential, serviced apartments or hotel. In order to be marketable, the majority of these units needed to be standardized and modularized, giving the necessary flexibility for the different uses. Current plans have committed to the units continuing as a pure residential project. Above this zone, where the area begins to drop away, a custom approach to the residential layouts begins. These floors are considered the 'luxury' units, being larger and more voluminous all the way until the last ten floors, where sizes increase with the single-floor 'penthouse' units.

The curved plan of the tower improves views past its densely located neighbours. The design allows for 85 per cent of the units to have water views – of the marina, or of the ocean beyond. The blades trace themselves from the ground all the way to the tip of this tower. They bend on the two most visible opposing faces, creating subtleties within these units on the two ends while the remaining units maintain their modularity. Beyond the lower two-thirds of the building, the blades on the two ends unify across the face of the building and continue to rise. They then allow for a unifying sculptural reading of the project to occur, with unit area fluctuations being more relaxed. As the modules drop off and the blades taper towards the heavens, the project becomes an Arabian sword with its sharp edge cutting the sky – raised in the air proudly above all the other warriors.

DAMAC Heights (second from right),
Ocean Heights (second from left)

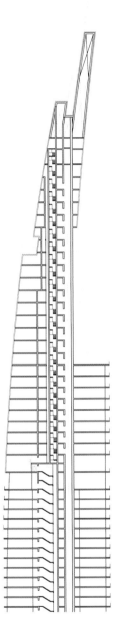

A typical unit plan after schematic design

Looking northwest from Dubai Marina

Boulevard Plaza

Dubai, United Arab Emirates
Status: Built (2011)
GFA: 60,927 m² (655,813 ft²)
Site Area: 17,200 m² (185,139 ft²)
Building Height: 173 m (568 ft)

The Boulevard Plaza Towers stand at the gateway to the Burj Dubai development. The importance of the site is further accentuated by being located immediately across the street from the tallest tower in the world – Khalifa Tower. The design strives to fit appropriately into this development as a respectful icon for the community.

The relationship of the forms and their articulation derive from both a contextual response and the building's symbol, representing a modern Islamic architecture set appropriately within the most modern Islamic city in the world – Dubai.

Despite the changing, curvaceous form of the building section, the units are modularized to standard layouts for construction simplicity, rationalization of space and cost efficiency.

While the modern Islamic feature façade patterns offer symbolism to address the context, they also acts as a sunscreen, which significantly reduces heat loads applied by the intense Dubai sunlight, thus reducing energy consumption produced by mechanical loads.

Over-sailing façades cantilever up to 5 m (16 ft), shading the east and west elevations, which contain a more transparent glass than the patterned north and south façades.

The podium is an open-air structure with natural ventilation and fans to help with air circulation. The open façade is clad with patterned metallic screens in between a monolithic colonnade that recalls the Islamic motif.

Northwest entrance gateway to Downtown

Main lobby, first tower

Photo detail, expressed fins

Precedent image

The first tower, looking towards
the Burj Khalifa

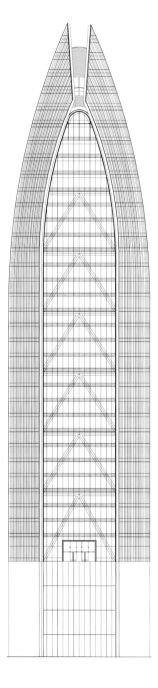

Second tower, west elevation

Aerial photograph from the Burj Khalifa

Crown geometry studies

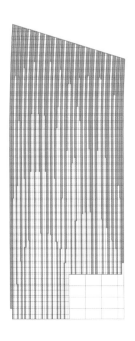

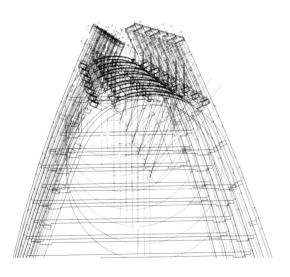

Long elevation

Northeast gateway entrance to Downtown

Vida on the Boulevard

Dubai, United Arab Emirates
Status: Construction Document
GFA: 92,000 m² (990,280 ft²)
Site Area: 7,361 m² (79,233 ft²)
Building Height: 243 m (797 ft)

As the second formal entrance to Downtown, the Vida development strives to define this node strongly as a 'gateway'. The Boulevard is a crescent thoroughfare which radiates around the centrepiece of the Burj Khalifa. The pressure on the Vida development is that it not only needs to reinforce the importance of this centrepiece, but it also has the responsibility of defining the entrance.

Consisting of two towers and a podium, the project explores a composition that optimizes views for the hotel and service apartments and presents a powerful expression appropriate to its gateway role. Although the towers are not the tallest objects on the Boulevard, their slenderness gives the edges a very strong vertical appearance. These edges are focused on the intersection, becoming the first visible elements on entering Downtown at this node. The towers are different heights, with Tower 1 pushing the structural limits (258 m/846 ft) closest to the Burj Khalifa and Tower 2 (133 m/436 ft) stepping down towards the intersection. The towers fan apart, engaging in a dynamic 'dance' and embracing their downtown role.

The heights of the towers are further extenuated by cutting through the podium all the way to the pavements. This was also considered important as it softens the tall podium street wall with the adjacent developments. The Vida wanted to present the entrance to Downtown as an inviting, human-scale experience. The podium also steps down towards this intersection, with terraces for the pool, and restaurants with views from the Dubai International Finance Centre (DIFC) to the Burj Khalifa.

A strong vertical expression was felt important, to anchor the development in its location across the Boulevard from the tallest tower in the world. As the Burj beyond dissolves into the haze of the sky, the Vida will strongly proclaim its role as the gateway to the Boulevard. The structure of the crown will remain sharply solid, while the vertical blades, reflecting the desert light, will seem to dissolve, giving the development a floating appearance.

View looking up from the podium

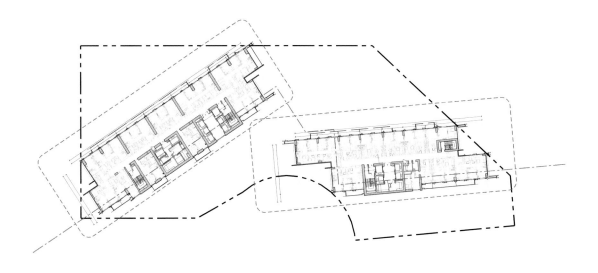

Typical plan for Tower 1 (left) and Tower 2 (right)

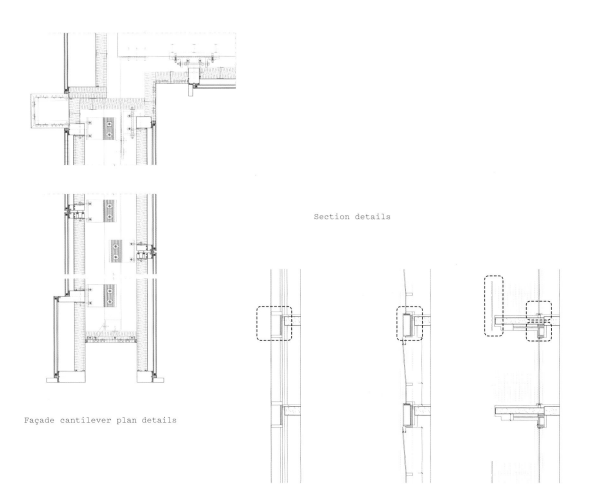

Section details

Façade cantilever plan details

Ubora Towers

Dubai, United Arab Emirates
Status: Built (2011)
GFA: 119,298 m² (1,284,113 ft²)
Site Area: 15,873 m² (170,856 ft²)
Building Height: 263 m (863 ft)

The Ubora Tower Complex is a mixed-use development located in the heart of Business Bay in Dubai. The design has given equal attention to its three different uses – office, residential and podium – in order to maximize their opportunities and viabilities within the site's context.

The office-tower position is rotated from the orthogonal at the street level to help focus the view from the office space down future sight lines towards the water and past the surrounding developments. As the tower increases in height, its four faces respond directly to their three-dimensional context. They all twist at varying degrees and angles to maximize available views.

The residential block deliberately does not compete with the surrounding towers in height, and instead keeps low and focused on the adjacent water body to the south. By designing the block as a linear bar rising from twelve storeys at the tower to fifteen storeys at the western end, a significantly greater percentage of units get an uninterrupted view of the water.

All three components are bound together by a 10,000-m² (108,000-ft²) public, densely landscaped deck that can be accessed from all three exposed sides of the project. Two monumental stairs lead up from either side of the office tower, with a third passing through a large 'gateway' within the residential block, down to the water's edge to the south.

East elevations, low residential block and tower

Looking east over Dubai Creek

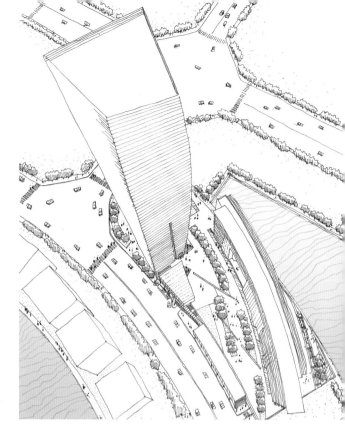

Sketch, looking down on to the podium

Looking west

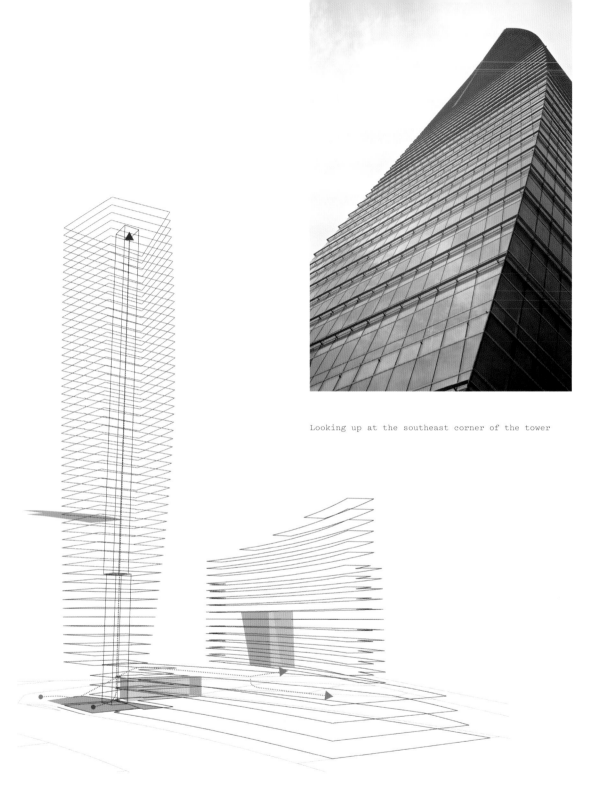

Looking up at the southeast corner of the tower

Diagram of the floor-plate geometries

North Star

Beijing, China
Status: Built (2010)
GFA: 161,780 m² (1,741,385 ft²)
Site Area: 2,525 m² (27,179 ft²)
Building Height: 107 m (351 ft)

Anchoring the overall development, this project engages the natural forces of the site and celebrates their potential. The project addresses the park as a 'quiet zone'. Its eastern face looks out at the main street's 'loud zone', and its northern civic edge relates to the masterplan corridor, where most retail and commercial functions are sited. The southeast corner of this site is linked to a future train station. The commercial and residential towers anchor each side of the site, and natural movement is caught between them. North Star's 100-m (330-ft) office tower stands on the intersection corner as a landmark, while the apartment tower is on the southwest corner, oriented towards the park and southern light. Daylight pours through skylights between the towers towards the ground, highlighting entrances on the north, south and west sides of the site.

The project is located on Beijing's Fifth Ring Road, close to the Olympic Park. To the west is a large leisure park and other cultural facilities, while to the east there are busy streets and a new subway station. Given this prime location, the project serves as an anchor for the larger masterplan, and links directly to the Beijing transit network.

Two twenty-five-storey office towers, 'the Rocks', are situated on top of a seven-storey mega retail podium. The two office lobbies are situated on the ground level, which are easily accessed from the street. The podium is designed as a 'retail experience', where people can sit and hang out as well as go shopping.

Flagship stores were placed on the two floor plates underneath the towers, while other shops were planned as small, rock-like forms, placed strategically in response to circulation flows from the surrounding areas. Paths inside the mall are planned like an artery system inside an organic body, or like running water flowing down a stream, which makes walking inside the mall a unique spatial experience. Externally, the different floor plates create terraces and stepped landscapes, where you can sit outside and enjoy the surrounding environment.

Northeast corner

Retail entrance, northwest corner

Office apartments facing south over the park

OPPOSITE South retail entrance

Looking upwards from the north entrance

Façade detail, east elevation

Ground level plan

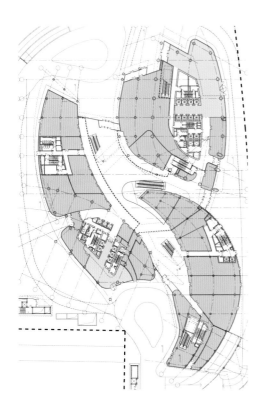

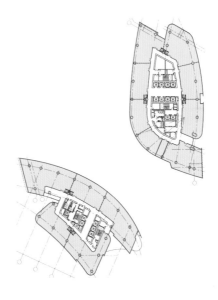

Typical tower plans

East elevation
OVERLEAF Interior retail

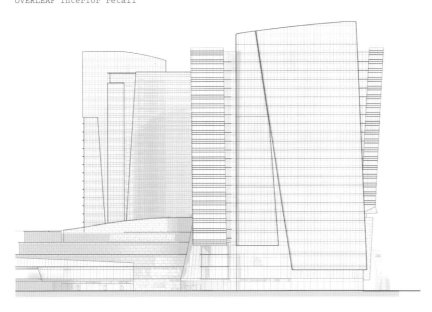

COLORADO: HOME IS WHERE THE HIKE IS

Cordillera Blanca, 5,500 m (18,000 ft) above sea level, Peru (1999),
by Andrew Bromberg. Journey: trekking up a glacier and sucking
on a lemon drop to resist altitude sickness.

No matter where Andrew Bromberg has lived, he has remained a
Denver Broncos fan, travelling back several times each autumn
from Asia to catch a game with his dad. 'It creates such a sense
of community here,' he explains. 'When I am in that stadium with
77,000 people, I just feel at home.'

Bromberg was born and raised in Denver, and as far back as
he can remember, living at the foothills of the Rocky Mountains,
he explored the mountains more and more. 'I felt safe up there,'
he recalls, 'but more than that, I just loved exploring, finding
this world, skiing the slopes.'

Bromberg did the same thing with his immediate neighbourhood:
'I somehow always loved climbing, even as a little kid. I
actually climbed every house in my neighbourhood. I picked up a
map of the subdivision where I lived and I would just knock them

off one at a time. I loved getting to a new place and seeing the world in a different perspective. Every house allowed me to understand my neighbourhood in a different way. You know, you could see the backyards that you could never see before, you could see that the steep streets that I thought were so daunting actually weren't so steep from up there.'

When asked whether that he meant he had a love for the residential landscape where he grew up, he shudders. 'I loathe the strip malls and cookie-cutter homes. They are just awful and they are the same everywhere. I would never want to live in that kind of environment. I just made the best of it as a kid.'

So what did he like? 'Well those [football] games, those were my first experience of a community. In a strange way it reminded me of going to Mecca. The city itself is so ugly, but once you get through all that and you are in the Holy of Holies, you are lost in the crowds, you are one, and you become larger than yourself. I don't mean to imply that I have a religious belief in the Broncos. I just think that when people come together for something, you create a larger world, and I always wanted to contribute to that.'

Venice, Italy (1993), by Andrew Bromberg. Journey: a tale of two cities, one on foot and one by gondola.

Bromberg's strongest memories, though, were of visiting his father's office downtown: 'My father used to work every Saturday morning in his office. Every Saturday morning I would want to go with him. I would hang out there, and I would spend the majority of the morning in his office, maybe thirty or forty floors up, with my head against the glass, looking down, fascinated with the landscape below. I was looking at rooftops trying to figure out how the mechanical stuff worked.

I was looking at people down there, fascinated by how their legs stick out when you're looking straight down on them from above. I couldn't get enough of it. I would just sit there with my head on the glass the entire time, watching the world below me. I guess I just have this urge to get up high and figure things out from there.'

When asked when he first became aware of tall buildings and their beauty, he says it was in Chicago. 'My mom is from there, so I remember going to visit my grandmother there for the first time on Lakeshore Boulevard. I was very young, and my memory of that visit was not the towers but the revolving door. On later visits I started to look up. To me what's fascinating about Chicago is it is an object-driven city: all these skyscrapers sit in the grid where you can see them on almost every side. If you compare that to New York, it is street wall-driven. I think I prefer the Chicago approach, even though the street wall is better for the urban fabric, it creates a continuous experience. I think I like being able to feel the space, but when you go to New York walls everywhere define you. Whereas in Chicago you move around corners and you have vistas that open up and collapse. Chicago has more opportunities for epiphany, more opportunities for the unexpected to happen.'

Does that mean he believes that architects should make the strongest possible objects and isolate them? There seems to be a contradiction in his work between his love of urban continuity and his desire to make recognizable objects. However, he rejects this. 'I don't think it is that simple. Think about the Flatiron Building, that triangular skyscraper in New York. Everyone I know loves the Flatiron Building. I believe that it's because you have something that is coming together, tying the fabric up in such a lovely way. It weaves these two streets, Fifth Avenue

> **'I would just sit there with my head on the glass the entire time, watching the world below me. I guess I just have this urge to get up high and figure things out from there'**

and Broadway, together. Talk about a simple building. It's pure and it's powerful. The Chrysler Building, the Empire State Building — those are amazing objects. But I don't think people really feel them at the street. When you go to the Empire State Building you look up and you only see the first tier because the tower steps back. You never actually experience the profile of the Empire State Building. But the Flatiron Building, you see it, it's there, right in front of you. You can embrace it, you can hold it. The same is true for the Tribune Tower in Chicago.' This could be seen as an object sitting by itself, but Bromberg points out that it's at the point where two routes come together: 'It makes sense of that space where Michigan Avenue crosses the Chicago River.'

An interesting question is whether this architect — whose work, at least as an independent designer, is all in Asia and on the Arab Peninsula — would like to design a skyscraper for his hometown. 'That's a really interesting question. What would I do?' Bromberg muses. 'I know I'd be relating whatever the

building was to elements of the environment that people in Denver understand, the mountains to the west, the sunset to the west. Would it be more monolithic, like the mountains, or would it spread out more? What would it look like from the street, and from the building itself? I don't know, but it would be really fun to try.'

Sandoval Lake in the Amazon, Peru (1999), by Andrew Bromberg. Journey: an early morning swim with caimans, piranhas and anacondas, immediately after this charcoal drawing was made.

Bromberg didn't stay in Denver because he felt the place was too limiting, but also because he had a certain wanderlust, which led him to backpack around Europe at a very young age and explore with little fear. He seemed able to make himself at home anywhere: 'The first time I got my driving licence, we came up to

Agrigento, Sicily, Italy (1993), by Andrew Bromberg. Journey:
steps beckoning to be climbed, explored and inhabited.

the mountains, three of us teenagers. We had a great day of skiing. Then on the drive back there was a blizzard, the highway was closed. So, we pulled into Idaho Springs, and discovered that my friend Darrin's father had a building he owned there. We knocked on the door and explained who we were. The guy managing the building gave us a room and blankets. We got back the next day and my dad asked us how it was; he'd never even noticed that we were gone all night, and that didn't seem extraordinary to me.'

Bromberg left Denver to study at Arizona State University in Tempe, then returned to the University of Colorado for his undergraduate degree. He left to attend the University of Washington and then the Southern California Institute

'I was free to move as long as I understood the rhythm and logic of the boats and of the tides and the weather. I had to be in tune with both the human and the natural landscape'

of Architecture before returning to Seattle, where he graduated with his master's degree and got his first job as a designer. 'I had a magical life there,' he recalls, 'especially once I moved on to a houseboat. It was leaky and very cold, but you were one with the water and the mountains in the distance. Lake Washington has locks that connect you to the ocean. At night, it is filled with fishing vessels that go through the locks in the morning and come back in the evening. But, there are always boats there – sailboats, fishing boats, motorboats. It was a working lake and that's what made it interesting to me. I had my sea kayak on that lake and I would wind my way through all that activity, and always with the mountains and the water and the sky around me. I was free to move as long as I understood the rhythm and logic of the boats and of the tides and the weather. I had to be in tune with both the human and the natural landscape.'

Despite his love for that scenery, he wanted more, and eventually accepted a job with Aedas, a large architectural firm based in Hong Kong. He was given the chance to establish a small atelier within the larger company. Bromberg was to be the 'high design' specialist, and he quickly obtained commissions in Dubai and then all over Asia. 'I went to Asia because I loved the culture,' he explains. 'I never expected to work there. Then I realized I was going to have this chance to do significant buildings in that part of the world, and that was very exciting for me. I just didn't have those chances in the United States. I also think I can do something different in Asia. There is a great deal of attention people give to how fast cities are growing and how architects there copy the West. I think there is something else going on there, because people appreciate nature in a way they do not here because of the urban density. They want to be near it and in it, and they want to feel it in their buildings. I connect with that.'

Jaisalmer, India (1995), by Andrew Bromberg. Journey: sunrise from a sleeping bag on a breezy rooftop.

Despite his clear love of cities, I suggest that he is really a mountain man, that he is in his element there, to which he responds: 'To me the mountains are special because you have a tree line. You're climbing and you're embedded in the pines, and you might catch a view every now and then. But then, all of a sudden, you're above the tree line. You have this incredible sense of space.

'One of the things, growing up in this environment, is that it made it so that scale doesn't intimidate me. Large cities or architecture don't overwhelm me. In fact, I love them. I became an architect because I want to make the world a better place and I want to do that in urban centres. I want to improve people's day-to-day lives in cities. In a city, you can impact many more people. I'm passionate about culture, I've always had an interest

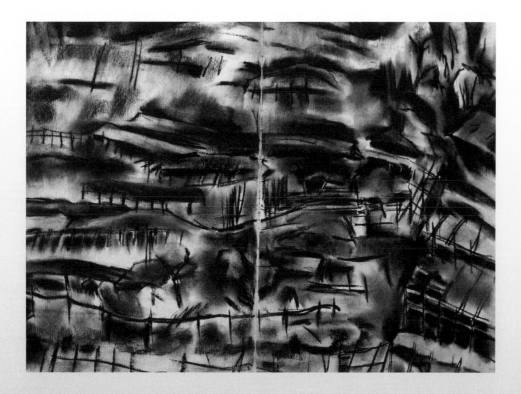

Below Ravello, Italy (1993), by Andrew Bromberg. Journey: hiking
up the stepped terraces from Atrani to Ravello, eating a lemon
picked from a tree to quench thirst.

in people and have many different passions. And I try to bring
it all together and balance it.'

However, he goes on to say that it isn't always easy to
achieve this balance. 'Sometimes I can be hiking and answering
an email, and then look up and realize I've been walking for
twenty minutes through a beautiful forest and I didn't even
appreciate it. That being said, I feel that forest no matter
what. I breathe that air and I feel the breeze; I can feel
tension being released even though I'm not consciously taking
in the forest at every moment.'

He refers to the particular landscape of the Rocky Mountains,
where he went hiking as a child, explaining that 'there are
three peaks of over 14,000 feet you can see from Denver: Pike's
Peak, Mount Evans and then Longs Peak. They're more accessible
than the ones further west, but they don't get as much snow.

The Rocky Mountains are very young, and that's why they're so rocky. Everyone thinks Colorado is filled with cold weather and snow. But you get sunshine 300 days a year. I did most of my hiking up here in the summer, but in the winter I would go further back. This is a landscape that really shaped me, that is embedded in my memories. It just fills me with joy.

'The journey is wonderful: never knowing what's around the corner, constantly having things reveal themselves. I've never been interested in having a space where the reaction is immediate'

'I never had a good sleeping bag for some reason,' he says, 'so I would be camping, freezing all night and I would wait for the light to come up and I would always be the first one out of the tent. I would go exploring around the sites where we camped, early in the morning. Collecting firewood, exploring, those are some of my fondest memories. My favourite parts were these huge boulders that had voids, really negative spaces, in them — we called it the caves — and they would let you go and disappear in there and explore and find your way out.

'You can really see the movement and the energy of the mountains if you follow the direction of the stone, the way they were uplifted by earthquakes, the way they lie against each other or jam in there. I love trying to imagine the forces that shaped all this. It's amazing to look at the fissures and lines in the rocks. Then you look more closely, and you can see those shapes in the mountains repeated in the rocks out of which they are made, they have such a sculpted nature to them, but one that comes out of forces that are so large, you just don't know what made them. It's way bigger than you, but you can touch them, feel them, get lost in them. I love how they relate to the sun. Some lichen only grow with certain orientation. It helps you figure out where you are.'

For this young architect, the mountains grounded him and lifted him up, both literally and figuratively. All his strongest early memories were tied up with the masses that tectonic forces had pushed up to loom above his childhood home and envelop him when he ventured into their arms. He had learned their contours, their valleys and their trails. He had made them his own, but they also owned him.

The question is how his love of this landscape continues to shape his work. 'Essentially, I like to move through space,' Bromberg says. 'If you look at most of the sports I've done – biking, kayaking, skiing – they're all about moving through spaces. I think I like to take it all in. It's about having things unveil themselves to you. And that builds a collective story, because I am talking about spaces that are large enough for us to experience together to contain us as we move through them, to reveal themselves to all of us. The journey is wonderful: never knowing what's around the corner, constantly having things reveal themselves. I've never been interested in having a space where the reaction is immediate. I like to have spaces that are always changing.'

This could sound like descriptions of pathways rather than spaces, but he disagrees, using an example from the mountain landscape of his home: 'Think about the tree line. One of the things I love about it is slowly getting above that line and seeing the ecosystem changing suddenly. Space opens up, and you get all these mountain flowers and different vegetation. It's not very subtle. You can actually find a line where everything changes. It's a line, there isn't much transition. Intellectually, I am not sure how that happens, but it is so clear. That sense of

Machu Picchu, Peru (1999), by Andrew Bromberg. Journey: looking down on the Temple of Sun two days after the southern winter solstice (23 June).

Machu Picchu, Peru (1999), by Andrew Bromberg. Journey: water
dancing between the steps, emanating from the cloud forest
above and on its way to the Amazon below.

discovery, and then space opening up, isn't that just amazing?'

Did he want to make buildings that worked in that manner? 'That is too simple and direct. I don't think you can make an immediate analogy. I want to open things up, that's for sure. I believe people are conditioned to certain patterns, whether they are urban patterns or experiential patterns. I believe it's very easy for people to make a routine and therefore not experience the world around them as much as they could. I do try to stretch that environment, twist it, pull it, to try and create some enlivenment, some awakening, some reaction.'

Bromberg seems neither to see his buildings as a human reaction to nor a version of the natural landscape, but rather as landscapes in themselves. He had never made the distinction between looking down from mountains or skyscrapers, discovering what was around the corner on a mountain path or a twisting street, or looking up at a wall of rocks or a street wall and finding in it the history of the place, sedimented into the veins of rocks or the patterns of use on a façade. He loved finding and making spaces that opened up after such journeys, and he liked it even more if he could create spaces of gathering where people could find beauty, meaning or just each other. 'When the founder of Singapore passed away,' he recalled, 'I was absolutely touched that what we designed as a retail space atrium at the bottom of the Star became a place where people gathered to mourn. They didn't see the shops around them, they saw a community space where they could gather, be together. It really touched me.'

Bromberg's buildings can seem to be many things at the same time: the result of his need to please clients, to motivate his design team, to make something he believes in, and to get them built on time and on budget. Beyond that, he is also trying to pack his buildings with ideas as well as forms, imbuing them with the complexity of the landscapes around them as well as the landscapes of his memory, all condensed into one structure and made to serve as an office building, convention centre, mall or church.

I asked Bromberg how he reconciles these conflicting demands, to which he replied: 'I would like to believe that I can create opportunities for everybody to find something they enjoy and get excited about in my buildings. It certainly was a struggle for me in school. When you're a student making a presentation, you have all these ideas you put into your design, as if it is your last one, and you want to talk about all of them. Then the professor says "pick one strong idea, you have too many things going on here". That's something I never agreed with. Even now I do that same thing. It's always multi-levelled for me. With a client, I don't have to explain the poetry of the space if that's not what they're interested in. They care about the efficiency, so with them I'm going to talk about how this enables that to work and fits together with this, and how it all comes together in that way. What I'm enjoying about the design, what I think people will enjoy when they go to the building, I don't have to bring that up to the client if it's not what they are interested in. I really do believe that you can have a multiplicity of readings in a scheme and still have a coherence to it. Not only that, but I think that a slight ambiguity in form or in space, something you can't quite figure out why it is there or what it is doing, that is good; it adds a richness to the project. I think the purity of an idea can sometimes be great. But I always ask, does that pure idea accomplish everything you want? In the end, I always try and have some purity, but at the same time I'm not afraid to deviate. I'll break the pure form, the one space, the big idea apart almost as soon as I have first designed it.

Kathmandu, Nepal (1995), by Andrew Bromberg. Journey: prayer flags blown by the wind, filling the valleys below, and the bike path back into town, with compassion.

That is why my buildings are so complex, because I want to do many things at the same time.'

When asked about the underlying logic behind all those ideas, he continues: 'It's ultimately about experience. Professors in school always cut me off, because I would be describing my projects, talking about how when you walk in you're going to see this and you're going to feel this. And they would say "hey, hold on now, you don't know what you're going to feel that day or what you're going to see". That bothered me a lot, because I believe that movement and perception of space are the most fundamental aspect of what we have to design into buildings. So that's when I started studying Gestalt theory and how we perceive figures. I came to understand that there are some responses that are universal, some forms and spaces to which we all have the same or similar reactions. That means in turn that you can set up expectations and rhythms.'

'I'll break the pure form, the one space, the big idea apart almost as soon as I have first designed it. That is why my buildings are so complex, because I want to do many things at the same time'

That sounds sweeping: does he really believe in absolute truths or facts about how you could evoke a particular reaction? 'Sure,' he says. 'Some people are more interested in one thing or the other, some people see different things, I find that very interesting in itself; it makes me want to make complex buildings even more. Yet I think that there probably is an aspect of the human being that is universal. There are not many people who can go into St Peter's in Rome and not be taken up by that space. There are not many people who can go to the Grand Canyon and not be blown away by it. So yes, I think that there is a universal aspect to what we experience in space, but at the same time I know that people have different reactions to what is within, before or around that space, and that is what I want to build into my buildings as well. I would like to believe that I can create opportunities for everybody to find something they enjoy and get excited about when they come to the buildings I design.'

Bromberg seems to have set himself a clear goal: to somehow, bit by bit, space by space, building by building, recreate the feelings and experiences he had as he explored landscapes — to condense them, to make them as layered in scale and parts as the world he saw around him when he was growing up. He did not care what the functions were for which he designed — nor, ultimately, who the clients were. He wanted to use whatever tools were at his disposal, opportunities were given and site he found to create those pathways of discovery. And at the end, somewhere in the heart of the building, whether at the base of the Kowloon Station, in the middle of a shopping mall or in a jungle nestled in an office building, should be that space where you are in awe.

'Journey: freedom of choice and an invitation to travel, explore, discover and increase awareness of our surroundings, our cultures and ourselves'

Chengdu City Music Hall

Chengdu, China
Status: Concept
GFA: 111,705 m² (1,202,383 ft²)
Site Area: 23,255 m² (250,315 ft²)
Building Height: 34 m (112 ft)

Chengdu City Music Hall will gather world-class music culture and art exhibition facilities and resources to become the city's new cultural landmark, putting the city on the map as one of the leading cultural capitals in the world.

The region has a subtropical monsoon climate with high humidity levels, ideal for abundant bamboo growth. Bamboo manifests here as lush vegetation on the rooftops and as the building's fenestration material, visually tying the whole complex together. The solid elevations are constructed of recycled traditional blocks echoing Chinese antiquity.

The scale and height of the complex's different components have been carefully considered to address ease of access for specific user groups. The civic components are more prominent in scale but they cascade down like Sichuan's water terraces to offer the public stepped access to the floating rooftops above. Smaller residential units are placed towards the nearby Jinjiang River, while an art-themed hotel, accessible from the roof gardens as well as the drop-off areas on the ground level, anchors the northeastern corner of the site.

Chengdu City Music Hall is interconnected via a series of pedestrian walkways meandering through the valleys of buildings like flowing rivers in traditional Chinese landscape paintings.

Rendering, the canyon between venues (on the left)
and the school of arts

Aerial rendering looking north

Rendering, inside the canyon looking west

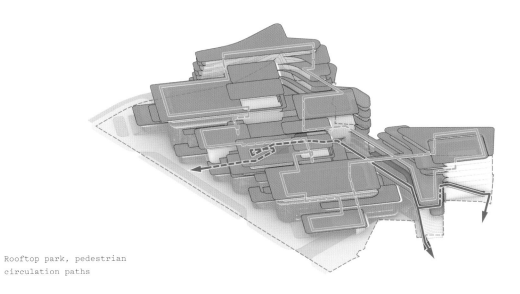

Rooftop park, pedestrian
circulation paths

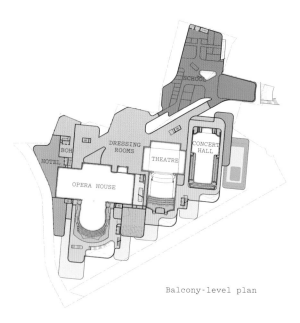

Balcony-level plan

Cross-sections through the small theatre (top)
and concert hall (bottom)

+34.0 m   +34.0 m

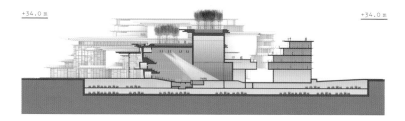

+34.0 m

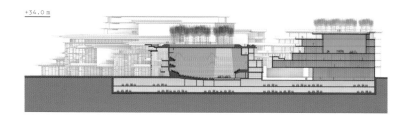

East performance plaza

Rendering, bamboo park on top of the opera house
fly-tower

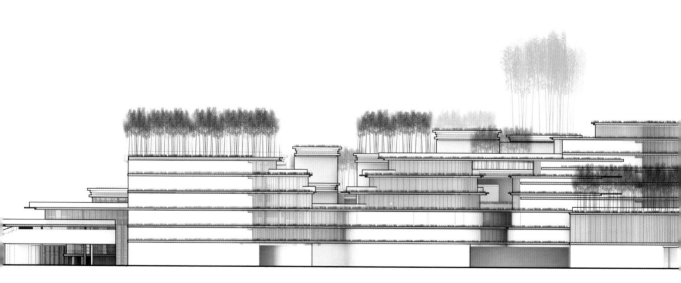

North elevation

Venue entrances at street level

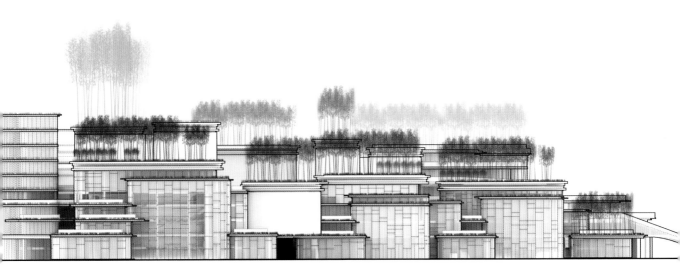

South elevation

The entrance to the school of arts in the east
performance plaza

Concert hall foyer

Opera house foyer

Winspear Completion Project

Edmonton, Canada
Status: To be completed 2020
GFA: 4,500 m² (48,438 ft²)
Site Area: 3,485 m² (37,512 ft²)
Building Height: 40 m (131 ft)

The Winspear Completion Project is the final phase of the Winspear Centre, which first opened in 1997. The current facility is home to the Edmonton Symphony Orchestra, with a 1,700-seat performance venue. The Completion Project will conclude the long-term vision of the Centre by expanding its performance capabilities with an additional 600-seat Music Box. It will also fulfil a desire to further integrate the Centre with the surrounding community by expanding and providing music-related facilities, studios and classrooms.

The project is a combination of renovating and expanding the existing building with a new facility to be built in an adjacent parking area east of the current facility. One challenge was how to tie the 'formality' of this entrance of the existing performance venue, whose lobbies are located on the west, to a more informal, inviting addition to the east.

The project has introduced three more pre-ticketed nodal events beyond the existing lobby of the Centre. The 'Link' will be a connection above the existing roof of the south elevation, which forms a highly open and visible link from the main lobby to the new addition. An escalator will bring people straight up from the public foyer of the lobby to a level-three link, which will be programmed with lounges, events and classrooms as a connection to the east.

The Link connects to the third node of the Centre – the 'Living Room'. This space is intended to be an inviting, semi-public zone that can be used both day and night, during performances or out of hours. The Link first connects to an amphitheatre, carved into an existing studio, and opening it up with views of an elevated garden. The 'Garden' is deliberately placed on the southeast corner of the site to maximize visibility and sunlight. The entire Living Room is focused on to the Garden. Beyond the amphitheatre to the west, there is a café area located on level two, which is the bottom of the amphitheatre and the Music Box foyer on level three, which is the same level as the Link.

The Music Box itself will have an automated seating system, an operable wall opening up to the foyer, and glass clerestories allowing for a strong connection to the outdoor environment. The smaller venue enhances the richness of the Centre with a more relaxed and inviting atmosphere than the larger venue, but one which meets the world-class acoustical quality for which the Winspear is recognized.

Aerial rendering of the southeast corner

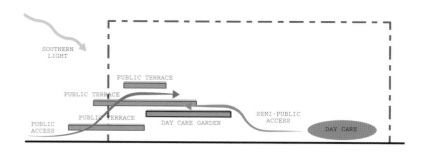

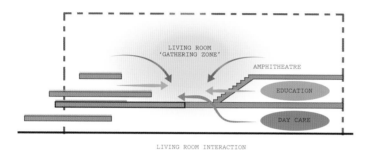

Interaction diagrams

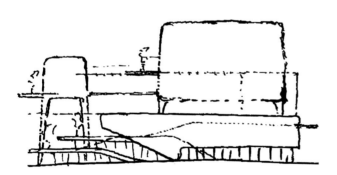

Interview concept sketch
by Andrew Bromberg

Living Room daylight studies

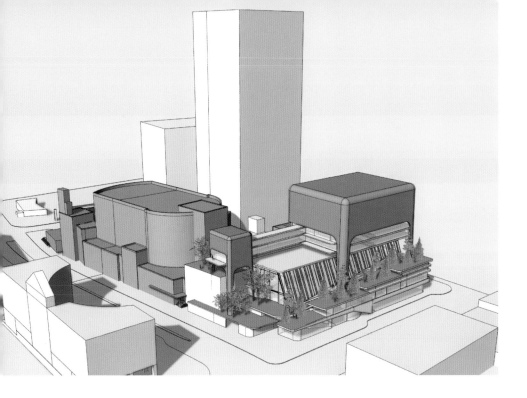

Computer massing studies,
looking northwest

Computer massing studies, looking southwest
OVERLEAF Living Room

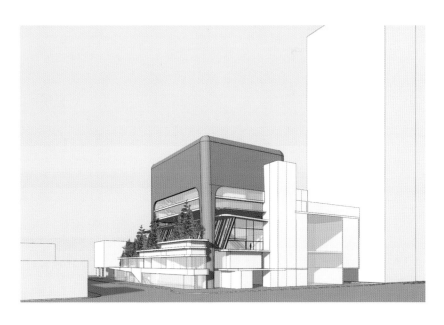

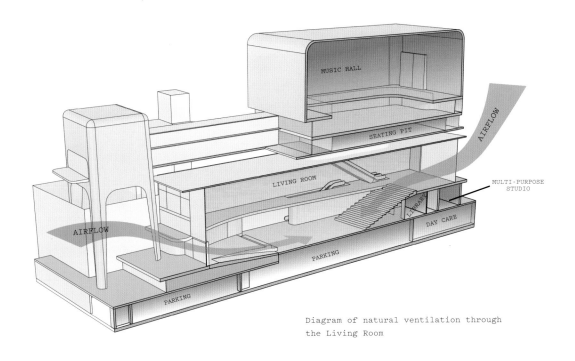

Diagram of natural ventilation through the Living Room

Circulation diagram through the Living Room

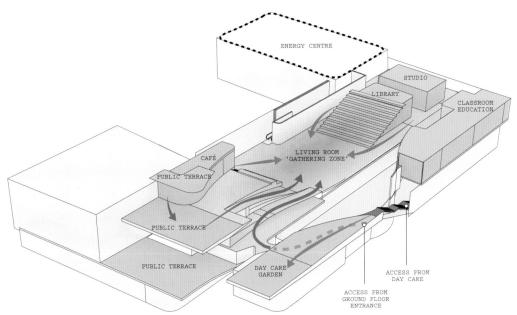

Street-level view, southeast corner

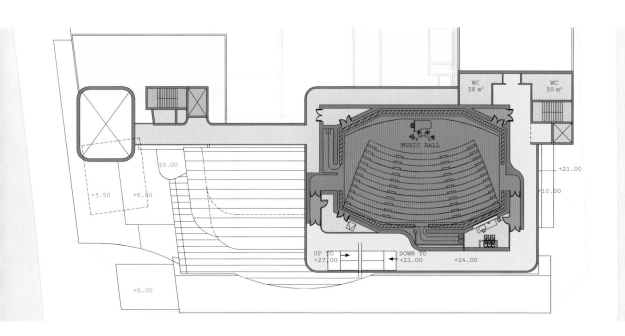

Venue stage level plan

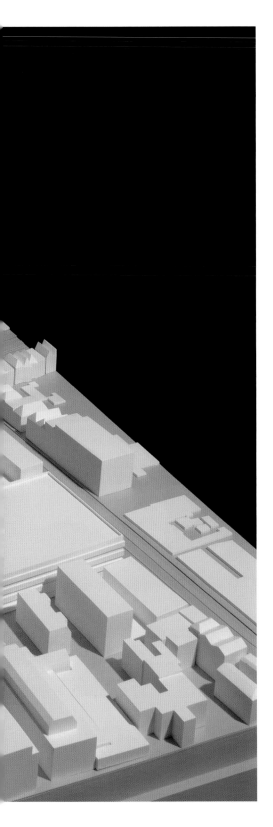

Dance and Music Centre

The Hague, Netherlands
Status: Concept
GFA: 47,210 m² (508,164 ft²)
Site Area: 5,969 m² (64,250 ft²)
Building Height: 69 m (226 ft)

The location of the project is right on an important, albeit under-utilized, urban square – the Spuiplein. This raises concerns of how to improve activity in this 'urban room', as well as how to achieve the transition between the public realm and the centre itself. The facility contains a range of uses, from the semi-public components of retail and box-office facilities, to the performance venue foyers, and finally to the five venues themselves. Adding even more richness to the programme is the fact that the centre also houses semi-private facilities for the highly respected resident orchestra (Residentie Orkest) and the highly regarded professional dance company (Nederlands Dans Theater). Added into this mixture is the Royal Conservatory, which itself contains four individual schools (three focused on music, and the other on dance). The design weaves a semi-public path through the entire facility, revealing the inner workings of what goes into these performances as well as how the artists develop. It is not only about the venues but also the studios, rehearsal rooms, classrooms and even the lounges. The students intertwine with the professionals, which on one level appears to be a completely supportive relationship, but can also appear like a 'battle' on the street level. Meanwhile, the professionals in their studios face off in a duel across the atrium with the students in theirs. However, the vitality of the centre depends entirely on how the public and semi-public components of the project engage with each other. With a limited site area for the requirements, facilities needed to be stacked, and the three distinct zones – public, semi-public and private – become the major organizational and focal volumes in the project.

Competition model, looking east

Rendering, view from urban
lounge, looking up

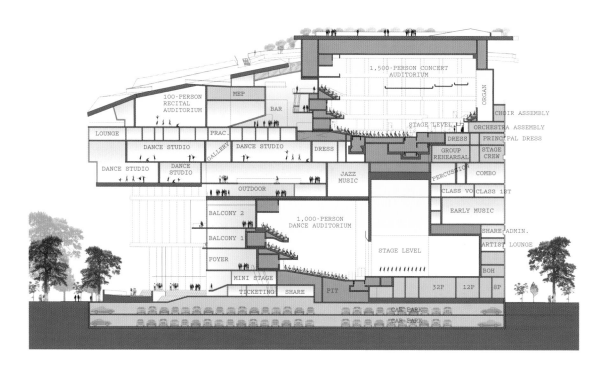

Longitudinal section through stacked
performance venues

Sketch view from Spuiplein plaza,
looking east

Concept diagram, semi-public flow

Rendering, street view, looking south

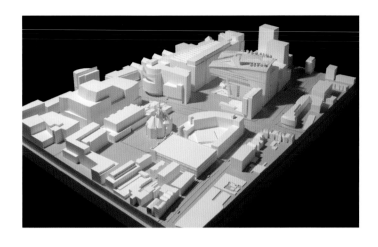

Competition model, looking northwest

Competition model, looking north

Rendering, looking northeast

Rendering, grand foyer

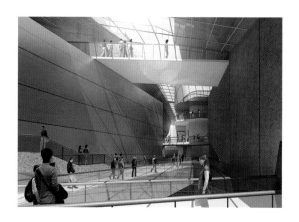

Rendering, looking south

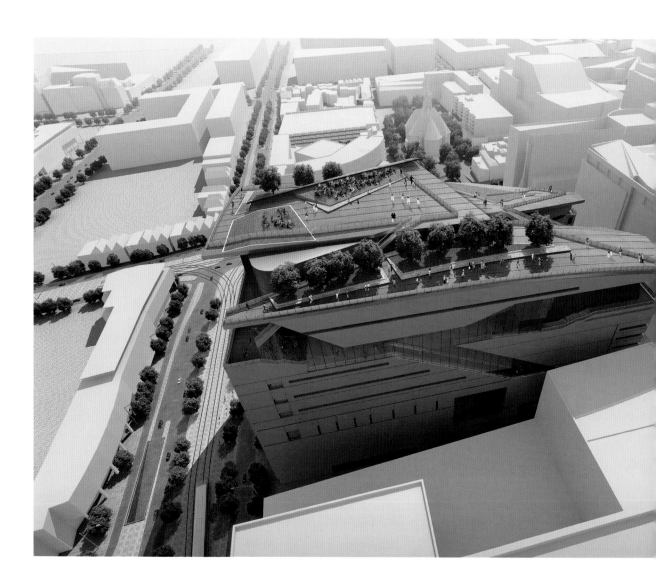

Competition model, detail of urban lounge

The Zheng He Cultural District

Nanjing, China
Status: Concept
GFA: 163,509 m² (1,759,996 ft²)
Site Area: 226,260 m² (2,435,442 ft²)
Building Height: 35 m (115 ft)

Located on Jiangxinzhou Island in Nanjing, the Zheng He Cultural District explores a meaningful tribute to a historic explorer of Nanjing, Zheng He, taking an approach of education rather than imitation. Zheng He made seven seafaring trips in the 15th century, from Nanjing to the eastern coast of Africa. The 25-hectare (62-acre) site is strategically located facing Nanjing city on an island masterplanned to be an eco-environment.

With a mix of programmes ranging from culture to entertainment, the primary route of discovery is defined by an undulating path symbolic of the coastline Zheng He followed from East to West. This progression places uses specifically tied to location along the path, while allowing the other uses to merge slowly from one culture to another. The Eastern Node of the journey is defined by a 2,000-seat theatre with Zheng He-themed performances. The Central Node is defined by a cultural centre, which showcases all cultures. The Western Node contains the digital centre and flying theatre, continuing the journey of discovery to the next frontier.

The East–West path becomes an open-air cultural museum, blurring elements that are influenced geographically, such as masonry, sculpture, vegetation, language and so on. The uses evolve as one moves through the project, with the only place that is 'whole' being the Eastern Node, which relates to Nanjing. Otherwise, the journey slowly transitions through different geographies as one moves west.

Located in its 'eco-environment', the project also blurs the line between built form and nature. The entire museum is outdoors but it is shaded from the sun, protected from the rain and designed to induce natural breezes. From the river, the project rises like green hills along a coastline. The 'cloud' becomes the unifying gesture which ties the project together, enables the environmental aspirations to be realized, and symbolizes the one constant an explorer by sea must experience – the horizon in the distance.

Rendering, view looking north over the rooftop gardens

East elevation (top),
west elevation (bottom)

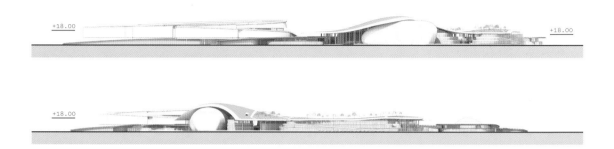

+18.00   +18.00

+18.00

Competition model

Rendering, plaza view, looking south

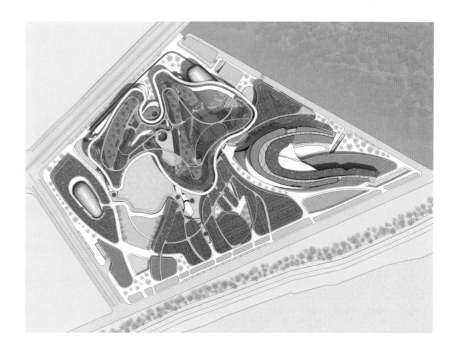

Roof plan

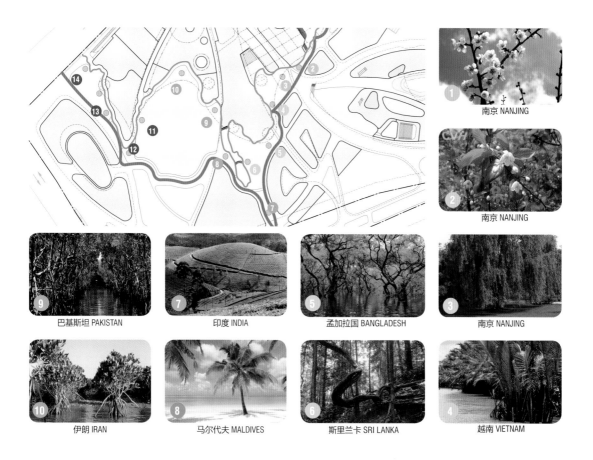

南京 NANJING

南京 NANJING

巴基斯坦 PAKISTAN

印度 INDIA

孟加拉国 BANGLADESH

南京 NANJING

伊朗 IRAN

马尔代夫 MALDIVES

斯里兰卡 SRI LANKA

越南 VIETNAM

Rendering, outdoor museum

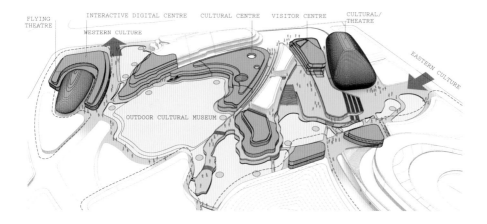

FLYING
THEATRE
INTERACTIVE DIGITAL CENTRE
CULTURAL CENTRE
VISITOR CENTRE
CULTURAL/
THEATRE
WESTERN CULTURE
EASTERN CULTURE
OUTDOOR CULTURAL MUSEUM

Axonometric plan, East-West Museum of Culture

Rendering, outdoor amphitheatre

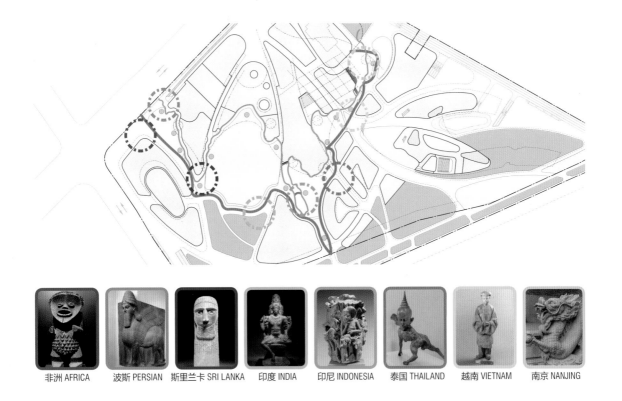

非洲 AFRICA   波斯 PERSIAN   斯里兰卡 SRI LANKA   印度 INDIA   印尼 INDONESIA   泰国 THAILAND   越南 VIETNAM   南京 NANJING

Journey, arts and culture sequence plan

Rendering, internal aquarium view

Rendering, canyon view looking towards the aquarium

Project (Re)Plant

Borneo, Malaysia
Status: Concept
GFA: 8,500 m² (91,493 ft²)
Site Area: 100,000 m² (1,076,000 ft²)
Building Height: 58 m (190 ft)

Project (Re)Plant is located in Borneo's natural wildlife reserve. The proposal is to improve the existing reservation and its paths, parking structures and various facilities by blending them into the landscape, minimizing environmental impact. The architecture is muted, allowing nature and its inhabitants to be witnessed undisturbed. As a result, the visitors' experience is heightened and more in tune with the habitat, providing an ideal platform for delivering education on wildlife conservation and protection.

When visitors arrive at the park they will leave the city behind them and enter a world immersed in nature. They will feel themselves to be in a new realm immediately thanks to the significant change of environment. The initial road journey meanders around the natural landscape topography, heightening a sense of anticipation and excitement. Car parks and arrival buildings are hidden below human-made hills, lushly vegetated to blend with the natural surroundings. These structures are open to the sky and surrounding views to encourage free flow of natural ventilation. Users are closer to nature as a result.

From the visitor centre, users journey further along the 'Educational Walk', which is a path that showcases the park's various plant and animal species. Walkways, travelators and bridges are elevated to ensure minimal disturbance of the environment. The animals can be observed in their natural state, roaming freely under – and in some cases over – the journey sequence. Further from the main walkways you can break away from the Educational Walk to more isolated zones and experience nature more intimately on cycling/walking trails, jogging/walking trails, forest trails and waterfront boardwalks.

Positioned along the Educational Walk are various nodes housing classrooms, cafés, lecture halls, sunken gardens and an aviary. These nodes are also open to the sky and along an elevation to provide natural ventilation and cooling. Classroom facilities will house workshops designed to educate visitors on wildlife and conservation. Visitors are also encouraged to climb up to look out over the majestic reservation from a completely unique vantage point.

Rendering, looking northeast

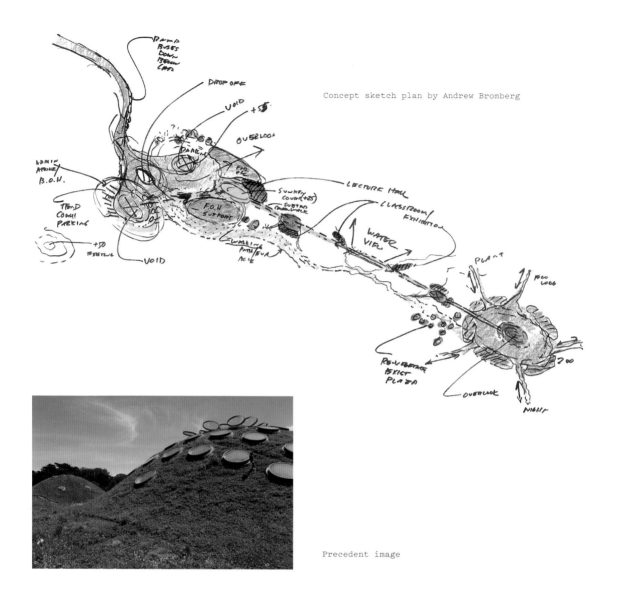

Concept sketch plan by Andrew Bromberg

Precedent image

Concept sketch elevation by Andrew Bromberg

Rendering, Educational Walk travelator

Rendering, safari view, towards classrooms

LOOKOUT
CLASSROOMS

TOURIST
CENTER

EDUCATIONAL
WALK

Rendering, visitor centre and classrooms

Rendering, Educational Walk safari journey

Long section through 'hills' parking and visitor
centre, showing the natural ventilation

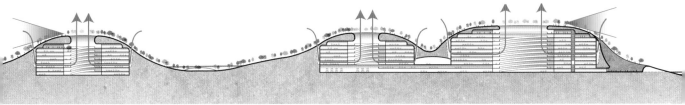

Rendering, entrance gateway

HQ Beer Garden

Hangzhou, China
Status: Concept
GFA: 164,205 m² (1,767,488 ft²)
Site Area: 88,526 m² (952,886 ft²)
Building Height: 60 m (197 ft)

Inspirational – the first word that comes to mind when contemplating an approach to this project. It is not often that one finds a client, a brief and a site that are so aligned with a desire to improve the lives of the people who will spend their precious time in the facility.

The client is known well for their philosophy of putting their people first. These employees are considered their greatest commodity and all efforts to improve their day-to-day lives are made whether in the form of training or amenities. It is understood that business productivity is fed through the social interaction of their employees. The approach to this design is to harness activities, inter-mix circulation patterns and blur boundaries between the most public of spaces and the most private of enclosures. Without sacrificing efficiency, this new network of interactive spaces and events becomes a new model of business which is as fluid and ephemeral as the client is as a world-leading techfin company.

However, social interaction is not a new concept in China, where courtyards have been utlized as one architectural approach for thousands of years. The Hakka villages are wonderful examples of these spaces, whose courtyards have no beginning and end as they are circular in nature. This is the client, a collective of talents that behave more as a family village than a corporate enterprise.

The brief is for a new headquarters. To differentiate a headquarters from a speculative development, this will be their home. Programmes to help encourage growth and maintain health and happiness have been provided. These include everything from restaurants, convenience stores and childcare to fitness centres, spas and even a florist.

Located in Hangzhou, one of the most beautiful cities in the world, the site is within the forested eastern slope of the hills bordering the western edge of Westlake and used to be home to a beer manufacturing facility. It is immensely beautiful, pure and inviting. The project strives to meld the aspirations into an environment that elates, soothes and inspires the senses with interactions, discoveries and journeys within the site and beyond into the inviting hills of Hangzhou's uplifting natural environment.

Competition model, looking northwest

Concept sketch by Andrew Bromberg, green space repair

Green terrace   Sunken plaza   Roof valley

Rendering, sky garden 'tree walk', looking north

Rendering, looking north

Roof plan, interconnected sky gardens

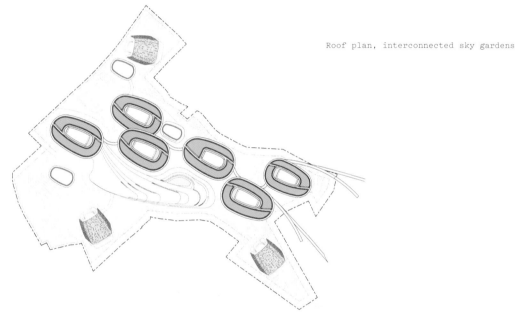

Precedent explorations

Rendering, concourse within office block

Rendering, view from 'tree walk' circulation

Concept by Andrew Bromberg, circulation diagram

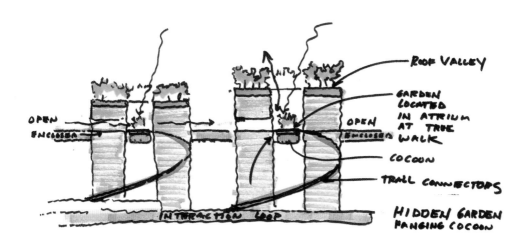

Biographies

Andrew Bromberg (RIBA, Assoc. AIA) is Global Design Principal at the international architectural practice, Aedas. Originally from the United States, he has been steadily gaining recognition for his ground-breaking architectural design for projects in China, the Far East, the Middle East, Europe and North America, ranging from smaller cultural, retail and educational venues to larger mixed-use commercial developments, as well as significant infrastructure and transport schemes.

Bromberg received his master's degree in architecture at the Southern California Institute of Architecture and University of Washington after completing his bachelor's degree in Environmental Design from University of Colorado and Arizona State University a few years earlier.

A keen hiker and traveller from a young age, Bromberg draws inspiration from his appreciation of nature and interest in how people live in different cultures around the world for creating meaningful, people-centric architectural works.

Aaron Betsky is dean of the Frank Lloyd Wright School of Architecture and a former practitioner, critic, curator and museum director. He has been deeply engaged with the world of architecture for almost fifty years and is the author of numerous monographs.

Competitions

2017
1st Prize (shared) Redevelopment of World Trade Center, Brussels, Belgium

2016
1st Prize China World Trade Center Phase 3C Development, China
1st Prize R501 Integrated Hub, Southeast Asia

2012
1st Prize Alibaba Mixed-Use Project Development, Chengdu, China
1st Prize Huawei Chengdu Mixed-use Development, Chengdu, China

2011
1st Prize Daxing Xihongmen Mixed-use Development, Bejing, China

2010
1st Prize World Twin Towers, Chongqing, of China

2009
1st Prize Express Rail Link West Kowloon Terminus, Hong Kong
1st Prize CX-2-1 (Sandcrawler), One-North, Singapore

2007
1st Prize Pazhou Exhibition Centre, Guangzhou, China
1st Prize Civic, Cultural & Retail Complex, Singapore

2006
1st Prize U-BORA Towers Complex, Dubai, United Arab Emirates
1st Prize Oceanscape Shams, Abu Dhabi, United Arab Emirates
1st Prize Solidere Development Block 20, Beirut, Lebanon

2005
1st Prize Ocean Heights Two, Dubai, United Arab Emirates
1st Prize Grand Marco Polo Hotel, Bejing, China
1st Prize The Legs, Middle East
1st Prize Jebel Hafeet Hotel, Al Ain, United Arab Emirates
1st Prize Khaldeya Mixed (Dancing Tower), Abu Dhabi, United Arab Emirates
1st Prize Xian Residential Development, Bejing, China
2nd Prize Dong Zhi Men Mixed-use Development, Xian, China

2004
1st Prize Ocean Heights Residential Tower, Dubai, United Arab Emirates
1st Prize Sunshine 100, Residential Development, Chongqing, China
1st Prize DAMAC Headquarters, Dubai, United Arab Emirates

2003

1st Prize North Star Mixed-use Development, Bejing, China
1st Prize Foshan Media Center, Foshan, China
1st Prize Goldfield San Lin Residential, Shanghai, China
1st Prize Zhongguan International Plaza, Beijing, China
1st Prize Workers Daily, Beijing, China
2nd Prize Luo Xi Residential Development, Guangzhou, China
Shortlisted West Kowloon Cultural District, Hong Kong

2002

1st Prize Szechuan Financial Corporation, Chengdu, China
1st Prize Beijing International Plaza, Beijing, China
Shortlisted Hong Kong Tamar Government Headquarters, Hong Kong

2001

1st Prize Chinese Overseas Bank Headquarters, Taipei, Taiwan

Selected Awards

2018

Architectural Review MIPIM Future Projects Awards: Commended, Cultural Regeneration: Chengdu City Music Hall

2017

AIA International Region: Honor Award for Open International, Architecture: Sandcrawler
MIPIM Awards: Winner, Best Futura Project: China World Trade Center Phase 3C Development
Architectural Review MIPIM Future Projects Awards: Commended, Retail and Leisure: China World Trade Center Phase 3C Development
Leading European Architects Forum (LEAF) Award: Winner, Future Building of the Year, Drawing Board: Chengdu City Music Hall
Architizer A+ Awards: Special Mention, Cultural-Unbuilt Cultural: Chengdu City Music Hall
World Architecture Festival (WAF): Finalist, Leisure-led Development, Future Projects: China World Trade Center Phase 3C Development
MIPIM Asia Awards: Gold Award, Best Chinese Futura Project: China World Trade Center Phase 3C Development
The American Architecture Prize: Winner in Architecture Design, Green: Chengdu City Music Hall; Winner in Architecture Design, Educational: Chengdu City Music Hall; Winner in Architecture Design, Mixed Use: Xihongmen Mixed-use Development
A' Design Awards: Golden Award: The West Kowloon Terminus Rail Link Project; Silver Award: Sandcrawler; Silver Award: Abdul Latif Jameel's Corporate Headquarters

2016

World Architecture Festival (WAF): Winner, Future Projects, Competition Entries: Chengdu City Music Hall
AIA Hong Kong: Merit Award, Unbuilt / Other: Chengdu City Music Hall

2015

The International Architecture Award: Winner, The Chicago Athenaeum: The West Kowloon Terminus under the Hong Kong Section of the Express Rail Link project; The Chicago Athenaeum: Water Park
Architectural Review MIPIM Future Projects Awards: High Commendation, Big Urban Projects: The West Kowloon Terminus under the Hong Kong Section of the Express Rail Link project
Leading European Architects Forum (LEAF) Award: Winner, Best Future Building of the Year, Under Construction: The West Kowloon Terminus under the Hong Kong Section of the Express Rail Link project
ARCASIA Awards: Mention, Category B-0, Public Amenity, Commercial Building: Sandcrawler
MIPIM Asia Award: Gold, Best Futura Mega Project: The West Kowloon Terminus under the Hong Kong Section of the Express Rail Link project
HKIA Annual Awards: Merit Award, Commercial Project Outside Hong Kong: Sandcrawler
World Architecture Festival (WAF): Finalist, Future Projects, Competition Entries: Project (Re)Plant; Finalist, Future Projects, Masterplanning: Project (Re)Plant; Finalist (Withdrawn), Future Projects, Leisure Led Development: Water Park

2014

AIA Northwest & Pacific Region Design Award: Honor Award: Sandcrawler
AIA Hong Kong: Merit Award, Unbuilt/Other: Alibaba "A" Community Development
The International Architecture Award: The Chicago Athenaeum: Guangzhou Commercial Showcase Complex
President's Design Award: Winner, Design of the Year, Built-in-Singapore Projects: Sandcrawler
MIPIM Awards: Finalist, Best Futura Project: Xihongmen Development; Finalist, Best Office & Business Development: Sandcrawler
MIPIM Asia Awards: Silver, Best Hotel & Tourism Development: Langham Place; Bronze, Best Mixed-use Development: Nanfung Commercial, Hospitality and Exhibition Complex; Gold, Best Office & Business Development: Sandcrawler
Cityscape Awards Architecture Emerging Markets: Winner,

Mixed-Use (Built): Nanfung Commercial, Hospitality and Exhibition Complex
A' Design Awards: Golden, Mixed Use: The Star; Golden, Retail: Nanfung Commercial, Hospitality and Exhibition Complex
ENR Global Best Projects Awards: Winner, Best Global Project, Retail / Mixed-use Developments: The Star
Quality Building Award: Merit Winner, Building Outside Hong Kong (Region outside Mainland China, Taiwan & Macau) Category: The Star
The Emporis Skyscraper Award: Top Ten: Nanfung Commercial, Hospitality and Exhibition Complex
World Architecture Festival (WAF): Finalist, Office, Completed Projects: Sandcrawler; Finalist, Hotel and Leisure, Completed Projects: Langham Place

2013
HKIA Cross-Strait Architectural Design Symposium & Awards: Silver Award, Shopping Centre: Guangzhou Commercial Show Case Complex
MIPIM Awards: Finalist, Best Shopping Centre: The Star
MIPIM Asia Awards: Silver Award, Best Retail and Leisure Development: The Star

2012
MAPIC Awards: Winner, Most Innovative Shopping Centre: The Star Vista
MIPIM Awards: Winner, Best Futura Mega Project: Express Rail Link West Kowloon Terminus
MIPIM Asia Awards: Winner, Best Chinese Futura Mega Projects: Xihongmen Development
World Architecture Festival (WAF): Finalist, Future Projects Leisure Led Development: Star Performing Arts Centre
Cityscape Awards Real Estate MENA: Winner, Commercial, Office & Retail Project Award, Built: U-Bora Towers
World Architecture News (WAN): Finalist, Transport 2012: Express Rail Link West Kowloon Terminus

2011
The International Architecture Award: The Chicago Athenaeum, Best New Global Design: CX2-1
MIPIM Asia Awards: Best Futura Projects, Gold Award: CX 2-1
World Architecture Festival (WAF): Finalist, Future Projects, Commercial: Fusionopolis 4
Cityscape Awards Architecture Emerging Markets: Winner, Commercial/Mixed Use Future: Fusionopolis 4; Winner, Leisure Future: Pazhou Exhibition Hotel
Cityscape Awards Real Estate MENA: Winner, Commercial Office and Retail Project Award, Built: Boulevard Plaza

2010
World Architecture Festival (WAF): Winner, Future Projects, Infrastructure: West Kowloon Terminus; Winner, Future Projects, Competitions: Dance and Music Centre
The International Architecture Award: The Chicago Athenaeum: Empire Tower
Architectural Review MIPIM Awards: Commended, Future Mixed-use: Civic, Cultural & Retail Complex
Cityscape Awards for Architecture in the Emerging Market:
Winner, Commercial/Mixed Use, Future Category: Civic, Cultural & Retail Complex; Winner, Tourism, Travel and Transport, Future Category: West Kowloon Terminus

2009
Cityscape Middle East Real Estate Awards: Winner, Future Projects Residential: The Pentominium
World Architecture Festival (WAF): Finalist, Future Projects, Commercial: Pazhou Exhibition Complex

2008
Architectural Review MIPIM Future Project Awards: Commended, Mixed Use: Arabian Performance Venue

2007
International Design Awards: Second Place, Architecture, Urban Design: West Kowloon Cultural District
Perspective Magazine: '40 Under 40', Andrew Bromberg

2006
Cityscape Architectural Review: Commended, Sport & Leisure: Jebel Hafeet
Architectural Review MIPIM Future Project Awards: Commended, Master Planning: West Kowloon Cultural District

2004
Cityscape Architectural Review: Commended, Master Planning: West Kowloon Cultural District; Commended, Residential Future Projects: Luo Xi

1995
American Institute of Architects Seattle Honor Award: Conceptual Work: Four Houses and a Bluff (selection Juror – Steven Holl)

1993
Rice University Fellowship, by Lars Lerup, Dean

1989
American Institute of Architects Colorado Anniversary Fellowship

1988
Dana Giffen Soper Memorial Fellowship

Project Credits

West Kowloon Station, page 26
Client: MTR Corporation Hong Kong
Project Manager: AECOM
Structural Engineer: AECOM, Buro Happold
M&E Consultant: Meinhardt,
Façade Consultant: ALT
Landscape Architect: EDAW
Quantity Surveyor: Windell
Main Contractor: Leighton – Gammon Joint Venture
Others: FMS, ROSTEK, MVA, Atelier Pacific
Project Team: Jonathan Ash, Jaenes Bong, Andrew Bromberg,
José Campos Macedo Gonçalves, Addison Chan, Andrew Chan,
David Chan, Ethan Chan, Gary Chan, Henry Chan, James Chan,
Jonathan Chan, Katherine Chan, Kocher Chan, Raymond Chan,
Tammy Chan, Timothy Chan, Vincent Chan, Ryan Cheng,
Stephen Cheng, Vincent Cheng, Cherry Cheung, Crystal Cheung,
Frankie Cheung, Gary Cheung, Jacky Cheung, Sam Cho,
Winnie Cho, Alan Chong, Jason Chong, Benny Chow, Keynes Chow,
Chun Kit Choy, Chun Yip Choy, Johnny Chung, Wai Chung,
Edward Cluer, Kenneth Crowley, Diogo Domingues Neto, James
Dowding, Kai Jian Du, Roger Dunn, Paul Empson, Duncan Fok,
Ken Fung, Vincent Fung, Axel Funke, Adrian Geaves, Keith Griffiths,
Shawn Hau, Cheri Ho, Kent Ho, Mantis Hon, Samantha Hu,
Philip Hui, Stanley Hui, Yann Hui, Matthew Ibarra, Beatries Ip,
Cliff Ip, Karl James, Reginald Keys, Jonathan Ko, Kenneth Ko,
Adrian Kwan, Gabriel Kwok, Keith Kwok, Sam Kwok, Jan Lai,
Kelvin Lai, Mandy Lai, Erica Lam, Kenny Lam, Ki Fung Lam,
Kingsley Lam, Mandy Lam, Wai Ming Lam, Alex Lau, Connie Lau,
Derek Lau, Kent Lau, Kenny Lau, Sarah Law, Eric Lee, Grace Lee,
Patti Lee, Ricky Lee, Ricky S. K. Lee, Terrance Lee, Ann Leung,
Edward Leung, Jackie Leung, Jerry Leung, Lawrence Leung,
Peggy Leung, Kim Li, Sam Li, Yvette Li, Francesco Lietti,
Jeffrey Lo, Karen Lo, King Po Lo, Salina Lui, Andy Ly, Thien Ly,
Chan Hong Mak, Matthew Mak, Jessica Man, Kenneth Man,
Wing Mang, Frank McGoldrick, Kai Mui, Paul Mui, Yuk Kei Ngan,
Meritxell Orti Andreu, Tobias Ott, Adrian Pang, Rosemary Pattison,
Mark Pollard, Karl Poon, David Prado, Frederico Ramos,
Jeremy Richey, David Robinson, Malcolm Sage, Scott Semple,
Elita Seow, Peggy Seto, Tony Sin, Melody Siu, Jennifer Sun,
Abigail Tam, Enoch Tam, Isabella Tam, Maggie Tam, Yin Tam,
Ambrose Tang, Danny Tang, Han Tang, Wai Tang, Winnie Tang,
Benjamin Thomas, Katrina Tsang, Paul Tse, Francisca Viegas Dias
Teixeira, Stephanie Vo Cong, Johnson Wai, Kai-li Wang, Yang Wang,
Richard Wilkinson, Brice Wong, Dicky Wong, Elmo Wong,
Gary Wong, Helen Wong, Jason Wong, Kam Chan Wong,
Samson Wong, Cora Wu, Alex Wu, April Wu, Ian Yeung,
Kristy Yeung, Angus Yip, Janie Yip, Jason Yue, Ada Yuen,
Anthony Yuen, Ching Yin Yuen, Kenneth Yung, Jack Zeng

Alam Sutera Residence, page 38
Client: PT. Brewin Mesa Utama
Project Manager: Arcadis Project Management Pte Ltd
Civil and Structural Engineer: PT. Davy Sukamta Konsultan
M&E Consultant: PT. Meltech Consultindo Nusa
Façade Consultant: ALT
Quantity Surveyor: Langdon Seah
Interior Designer: IPA
Architect of Record: Planning & Development Workshop
Project Team: Ira Agustina, Nyssa Amelia, Andrew Bromberg,

Henry Chan, Qisen Chen, Zoe Ho, Kevin Jose, Kevin Kasparek,
Kevin Kwok, Lawson Lai, Helena Lee, Patti Lee, Thien Ly,
David Prado, Jakub Riha, Yuan Tiauriman, Richard Tsang,
Hurakan Yeung, Gordon Yuen, Yundi Zhang, Jessie Zhong

China World Trade Center, page 42
Client: China World Trade Co., Ltd
Project Team: Andrew Bromberg, Cai Hongkui, Kevin Kwok,
Helena Lee, Jakub Riha, Jie Yuan, Gordon Yuen

Commerce Centre, page 48
Client: Confidential
Project Team: Jonathan Alotto, Andrew Bromberg, Benny Chow,
Kevin Kasparek, Kevin Kwok, Helena Lee, Patti Lee, Huko Ma,
Matthew Mak, Thien Ly

High Speed Rail, page 52
Client: Confidential
Project Team: Gruffudd Ab Owain, Andrew Bromberg,
Alen Nikolovski, Frederico Ramos, Yuan Tiauriman

Integrated Hub, page 56
Client: *Confidential
Project Manager: Arcadis
Structural Engineer: Arup
M&E Consultant: WSP
Traffic Consultant: Arup
Landscape Designer: ICN
Interior Designer: Aedas HK
Façade Consultant: Arup
Sustainability: Arup
Quantity Surveyor: RLB
Project Team: Gruffudd Ab Owain, Mohd Abdullah, Rafael Acosta
Nino, Julia Agonoy, Princess Mia Carla Villarica Aguilar,
Jonathan Alotto, Tony Ang, Trina Ang, Sava Atanackovic,
Caroline Aviles, Maria Aycardo, Alice Aye, Thinzar Aye,
Amrit Banerjee, Nittin Baskar, Lea Blasco, Leo Boey,
Jaenes Bong, Jacek Brodniewicz, Andrew Bromberg,
Christian Bulalacao, Audi Capellan, Paulo Cedo, Aileen Cervantes,
Ivan Chan, Olivia Chan, Daniel Chia, David Chim, Henry Chong,
Benny Chow, James Dowding, Arnel Elero, Dayu Fatsy Asyari
Djuanda, Christian Freitag, Joo Goh, Keith Griffiths,
Arthur Gunawan, Vamsi Gunturu, Paul Hamilton, Harold Hee,
Cai Hongkui, Eric Hoong, Junizza Husin, Kevin Jose,
Kevin Kasparek, Shu Wei Kuek, Lance Kum, Siva Kumaresan,
Kevin Kwok, Noe Lagamayo, Janis Law, Helena Lee,
Jasmine Lee, Patti Lee, James Leong, Simin Lin, Thien Ly,
Huko Ma, Mark Magno, Matthew Mak, Frank McGoldrick,
Lancelot Ng, Tobias Ott, Thao Tham Pham, James Pilapil,
David Prado, Jakub Riha, James Sagadewan Konna, Steven Shaw,
Joshua So, Wedha Suajaya, Adeline Suhadi, Isabel Tan, Yew Tan,
Danny Tang, Yuan Tiauriman, Ramon Villanueva Allen,
Hui Ee Wong, Gordon Yuen, Huiying Zhang, Yundi Zhang

**Nanfung Commercial, Hospitality and Exhibition Complex,
page 82**
Client: Nan Fung Group
Structural Engineer: Arup
M&E Consultant: JRP

Façade Consultant: Arup
Quantity Surveyor: DLS
Interior Designer: Aedas Interior
LDI: Guangzhou Design Institute
Main Contractor: Shanghai Construction Group General Co.
Project Team: Andrew Bromberg, Angela Chan, Billy Chan,
Henry Chan, Kevin Chan, Plato Chan, Allen Chau, Jennifer Chen,
Aidan Chong, Louise Chow, James Dowding, Sam Ki,
Eugene Kiang, Lawson Lai, Emily Lau, Leo Lau, Patti Lee,
Tiffany Leung, Katie Ng, Tony Sin, Jacky Tam, Jason Tang,
Richard Tsang

Ocean Heights, page 88
Client: DAMAC Gulf Properties LLC
Structural Engineer: Meinhardt
M&E Consultant: Ian Banham and Associates
Façade Consultant: ALT
Architect of Record: ECG Engineering Consultants Group
Main Contractor: Arabtec
Project Team: Karma Barfungpa, Andrew Bromberg, Candy Chan,
Henry Chan, Judy Chan, Pong Chan, Felix Fischer, David Fung,
Kevin Kasparek, Shun Lai, Edward Lam, Leo Lau, Helena Lee,
Peter Lee, Raymond Lee, May Leung, Andy Lu, Karl Poon,
Matthew Shao, Joshua So, Patrick Wai, Pong Wan, Lyla Wu, Albert Yu

Daxing Xihongmen Mixed-use Development, page 94
Client: Beijing Xing Chuang Zhidi Real Estate Development Co., Ltd
Structure: CCDI
MEP: CCDI
Façade Consultant: DADI
Interior Designer: BLD
Lighting Designer: BPI
Traffic Consultant: Aecom
Hotel consultant: Inproject
Retail Consultant: JLL
LDI: CCDI
Contractor: Wanxing Building Group & Xinxing Baixin Construction
Group
Project Team: Jonathan Alotto, Jaenes Bong, Andrew Bromberg,
Kevin Chan, James Dowding, Te He, Kevin Kwok, Janis Law,
Helena Lee, Patti Lee, Francesco Lietti, Thien Ly, Huko Ma,
Vienne Ma, Tobias Ott, David Prado, Jakub Riha, Danny Tang,
Jie Yuan, Kay Zhang

Plac Grzybowski, page 102
Client: Ghelamco Poland Sp. z.o.o.
Theatre and Acoustics Consultant: Artec Consultants Inc.
Project Team: Jaenes Bong, Andrew Bromberg, Benny Chow,
Joanna Chung, Kocher Hung, Stephen Kwok, Lawson Lai,
Helena Lee, William Lim, Matthew Mak, David Prado,
Yuan Tiauriman Henry Yue,

Cloud on Terrace, page 108
Client: Gemdale Properties and Investment Corporate Limited
Structure: Tianhua
Interior Designer: Woodsbagot
Lighting Designer: KGM
Substation Engineer: SEPD
MEP: China Team / Tianhua

Façade Consultant: Gaopen
LDI: Tianhua
Project Team: Jaenes Bong, Andrew Bromberg, Ivan Chan,
Benny Chow, Paul Hamilton, Cai Hongkui, Kevin Kasparek,
Kevin Kwok, Janis Law, Helena Lee, Patti Lee, Hung Keung Lo,
Huko Ma, Matthew Mak, David Prado, Jakub Riha, Kyra Swee,
Yew Tong Tan, Yuan Tiauriman, Hurakan Yeung, Jie Yuan,
Jason Yue, Yundi Zhang

The Star, 130
Client: CapitaLand Mall Asia Limited, Rock Productions Pte Ltd
Structural Engineer: Parsons Brinkerhoff
Civil and Structural Engineer: Thornton Tomasetti
M&E Consultant: Mott MacDonald
Theatre and Acoustic Consultant: Artec Consultants Inc.
Façade Consultant: ALT
Quantity Surveyor: Davis Langdon & Seah (S) Pte Ltd
Fire/Environmental Consultant: Arup Singapore Pte Ltd
Landscape Designer: ICN Design International
Lighting Designer: LPA
Project Team: Tony Ang, Caroline Aviles, Andrew Bromberg,
David Chan, Henry Chan, Olivia Chan, Thomas Chan, Wayne Chan,
Sam Cheung, Sam Cho, Alvin Choo, Allan Curr, Roderick Delgado,
Bryan Diehl, Muhammad Fadly, Petrina Goh, Emma Hardy,
Ka-Ming Ho, Samantha Hu, Yann Hui, Syarif Fahmi Ismail,
Koh Thien Nee, Willie Kua, Leo Lau, Helena Lee, Henry Leung,
Francesco Lietti, Isa Bin Lmin, Andrew Loke, Vicky Pang,
Boris Manzewski, Kenneth McGuire, Moreno Negri,
Lancelot Ng, Alen Nikolovski, Michael O'Brien, Tobias Ott,
Garry Phillips, Iskandar Rahman, Mario Sana, Eugene Seow,
Tony Sin, Joshua So, David Tan, Tan Chai Tan, Danny Tang,
Serene Toh, Jason Wang, Lukasz Wawrzenczyk, Ian Wigmore,
Kent Williams, Kenny Wong, Magdaline Yeo, Ada Yuen,
Sharifah Zerdharina

Sandcrawler, page 142
Client: Lucas Real Estate Singapore
Project Manager: Faithful + Gould Pte Ltd
Civil and Structural Engineer: Arup Singapore Pte Ltd
M&E Consultants: J. Roger Preston (S) Pte Ltd
Theatre and Acoustic Consultant: Arup Singapore Pte Ltd
Quantity Surveyor: Faithful + Gould Pte Ltd
Façade Consultant: ALT
Landscape Consultant: Adrian L. Norman Ltd
Building Maintenance Unit Consultant: E. W. Cox S. E. Asia Pte Ltd
Lighting Consultant: Lighting Design Partnership Pte Ltd
Façade Contractor: Permasteelisa Group
Main Contractor: Obayashi Singapore
Project Team: Tony Ang, Andrew Bromberg, Darren Chan,
Derrick Chan, Sam Cheng, Konrad Grabczuk, Ka-Ming Ho,
Kevin Kasparek, Willie Kua, Leo Lau, Helena Lee, Kenzie Lo,
Loo Soo Sing, Alen Nikolovski, David Tan, Maciej Setniewski,
Tony Sin, Kent Williams, Fiona Wong, Catherine Wu, Magdaline Yeo

Kortrijk, page 152
Client: Ghelamco Group
Architect of Record: Jaspers-Eyers
Project Team: Jonathan Alotto, Andrew Bromberg, James Dowding,
Kevin Kasparek, Helena Lee

Huafa Arts Center, page 156
Client: Zhuhai Huafa Investment Holdings Limited
Architect: Andrew Bromberg
Project Team: Jonathan Alotto, Andrew Bromberg, Henry Chan,
Thomas Chan, Benny Chow, Helena Lee, Thien Ly, Matthew Mak,
Yuan Tiauriman, Lawrence Ting

Abdul Latif Jameel's Corporate Headquarters, page 162
Client: Abdul Latif Jameel Company Limited
Structural Engineer: Aurecon Group
M&E Consultant: Clarke Samadhin Associates
Façade Consultant: ALT
Fire and Safety Consultant: Design Confidence
Landscape Design: Adrian L. Norman Limited
Lift Engineer: Cooper & Wilcock FZ LLC
Lighting Designer: Light Bureau AS
Environmental Consultant: Anthesis Consulting
Project Team: Zainab Abbas, Reem Abuzeid, Scott Albon,
Wael Al-Taweel, Aidan Alunan, Andrea Bernocco, Aileen Bongon,
Andrew Bromberg, Henry Chan, Irene Chin, Cass Choong,
Benny Chow, Gregory Chung, Natalie Chung, Martina Costantini,
Silva Da Silva Morais, Jesus De Jesus, Reynaldo Domingo,
Michael Fowler, Ben Ho, Alistair Hutson, Miranda Ip,
Jay Jocona, Christina John, Kevin Kasparek, Lawson Lai,
Vincent Lai, Helena Lee, Patti Lee, Cheryl Li, Ken Luk, Grace Lun,
Thien Ly, Logan MacWatt, Nishal Majeed, Matthew Mak,
Tom Mak, Simon Paddison, Nicolas Pare, David Prado, Kasif Rashid,
Yebin Sreenivasan, Iain Strudley, Damian Talbot, Yew Tong Tan,
Yuan Tiauriman, Jelena Tomic, Richard Tsang, Ashwin Vengayil,
Romeo Villa, Ryan Villareal, Guannan Wang, Florence Wong,
Jeff Wong, Sarah Wong, Veronica Wong, Jeremy Wu, Gordon Yuen,
Jieshan Zhong

Da Wang Jing Mixed-use Development, page 186
Clients: Beijing Kuntai Real Estate Development Group Ltd/Beijing
Yonghui Properties Ltd/China Aviation Planning and Construction
Development Co. Ltd/Beijing Meirui Tai Fu Properties Ltd
Meirui:
Structure Engineer: Arup
M&E Consultant: Parsons Brinckerhoff
Façade Consultant: Schmidlin
Landscape Designer: ACLA
Interior Designer: Gensler
Lighting Consultant: Isometrix
Traffic Consultant: MVA
Quantity Surveyor: WT PARTNERSHIP
Local Design Institute: CARB
Contractor: The Third Contraction Co., Ltd of China Construction
First Group
Kuntai:
Structural Engineer: Carb
M&E Consultant: Carb
Façade Consultant: Inhabit
Landscape Designer: Eco Land
Interior Designer: PAL Design Group
Lighting Consultant: Adcas
Local Design Institute: Carb
Contractor: The Third Contraction Co., Ltd of China Construction
First Group
Project Team: Andrew Bromberg, Benjamin Chan, Henry Chan,
Thomas Chan, Victor Chan, Kelly Chang, Toby Cheung, Benny
Chow, Xiao Duan, Clarence Fong, Lu Gan, Rui Ying Ge, Shirley Ho,
Yi Hu, Jenny Huang, Kevin Kasparek, Sam Ki, Anthony Ko,
Kevin Kwok, Lawson Lai, Wai Ming Lam, Helena Lee, Patti Lee,

Francesco Lietti, Diana Lin, Christopher Loh, Thien Ly, Huko Ma,
Matthew Mak, Peter Marshall, Nathanael Maschke, Katie Ng,
Tri Nguyen, Agarwal Paridhi, Zhen Shan, Ming Ze Sun,
Tiffany Szeto, Lawrence Ting, Yi-Ju Tseng, Emily Wang, Jun Wang,
Viktoria Wang, Yu Chen Wang, Allen Wen, William Wong,
Hurakan Yeung, Tak Yim, Mavis Yip, Jie Yuan, Jason Yue,
Hugo Zhang, Maggie Zhang, Jessie Zhong, Helen Zhou

DAMAC Heights, page 192
Client: DAMAC Gulf Properties LLC
Structural Engineer: Ramboll Group
Stuctural Engineer of Record: AECOM
M&E Consultant: Ramboll Group
M&E Engineer of Record: AECOM
Façade Consultant: Ramboll Group
Fire and Safety Consultant: Ramboll Group
Geotechnical Consultant: Langan Engineering
Interior Designer: JC Maclean
Landscape Designer: WAHO
Wind Consultant: RWDI
Main Contractor: Arabtec
Architect of Record: AECOM
Project Team: Jaenes Bong, Andrew Bromberg, Jason Chong,
Marcin Klocek, Helena Lee, Tobias Ott, Joshua So, Patrick Wai

Boulevard Plaza, page 196
Client: Emaar Properties PJSC
Structural Engineer: Hyder Consulting (ME) Ltd
M&E Engineer: Hyder Consulting (ME) Ltd
Façade Engineering: ALT
Interior Designer: Aedas Interior
Lighting Designer: Bo Steiber Lighting Design
Landscape Designer: Aedas Landscape
Architect of Record: Brewer Smith & Brewer Gulf
Main Contractor: Samsung C&T Corporation
Project Team: Hani-Al-Turk, Paul Blazek, Andrew Bromberg,
Gigi Chan, Pong Chan, Henry Chau, Jolish Chengammal,
Pooja Choudary, Ali Ghandour, Ei Kie Giam, Cedric Gonsalves,
Hemalika Gulati, Mohammed Hamdan, Tarek Bou Hassoun,
Renju Hiranmayi, Queenie Ip, Kevin Kasparek, Leo Lau,
Raymond Lee, Enrique Legaspi, Ada Leung, May Leung,
Wilson Li, Andy Lu, Ewa Maciejewski, Logan MacWatt,
Stephen Marsden, John Minford, Ewa Niescioruk, Rayk Paz,
Karl Poon, Tumanga Qholosha, Juan Barrera Rodriguez, Ivor Shing,
Tony Sin, Yebin Sreenivasan, Piotr Stachurski, Ida Sze, Jason Tang,
Patrick Wai, Albert Yu

Vida on the Boulevard, page 202
Client: Emaar Properties PJSC
Project Manager: Turner & Townsend
Lead Consultant: WSP Middle East Architectural & Engineering
Consultancy
Structural Engineer: WSP Middle East Architectural & Engineering
Consultancy
M&E Consultant: WSP Middle East Architectural & Engineering
Consultancy
Civil Engineer: WSP Middle East Architectural & Engineering
Consultancy
Quantity Surveyor: Ominium International Ltd
Interior Designer: FG stijl
Façade Consultant: WSP Middle East Architectural & Engineering
Consultancy
Landscape and Irrigation Consultant: Cracknell
Lighting Designer: Light Alliance
Project Team: Hugo Almeida Marques, Jonathan Alotto,

Andrew Bromberg, Ivan Chan, Reynaldo Domingo, Michael Fowler, Nikko Hilario, Alistair Hutson, Abhisek Karn, Kevin Kasperak, Simon Knight, Jinesh Kumar, Rachit Kumar, Kevin Kwok, Helena Lee, Kathrine Luna, Huko Ma, Nishal Majeed, Cristian Ramirez Llarena, Niha Sheikh, Yebin Sreenivasan, Damian Talbot, Danny Tang, Ramos Villa, Jason Yue

Ubora Towers, page 206
Client: Bando Engineering & Construction Co. Ltd
Structural Engineer: Ramboll Group
M&E Consultant: Ramboll Group
Fire & Safety Consultant: Ramboll Group
Façade Consultant: ALT
Wind Consultant: BMT Fluid Mechanics Ltd
Main Contractor: Bando
Project Team: Karma Barfungpa, Andrew Bromberg, Candy Chan, Henry Chan, Vivian Cheung, Julie Dubois, Sabine Fuehrer, Kevin Kasparek, Willie Kua, Edward Lam, Leo Lau, Helena Lee, Ada Leung, Francesco Lietti, Ewa Niescioruk, Max Ng, Maffrine Ong, Mirco Pieroni, Karl Poon, Tony Sin, Joshua So, Jason Tang, Patrick Wai

North Star, page 210
Client: Beijing North Star Land Company Ltd
Structural and Environmental Engineer: CEEDI
Project Team: Boran Agoston, Andrew Bromberg, Gigi Chan, Jennifer Chik, Helena Lee, Johnson Ma

Chengdu City Music Hall, 234
Client: Chengdu Urban Construction Investment Management Group Co., Ltd
Quantity Surveyor: Currie & Brown
Theatre and Acoustic Consultant: Arup
Project Team: Andrew Bromberg, Henry Chan, Benny Chow, Cai Hongkui, Kevin Kwok, Helena Lee, Yin Sheng Liu, Matthew Mak, David Prado, Jakub Riha, Yuan Tiauriman, Gordon Yuen

Winspear Completion Project, page 244
Client: Stantec
Theatre and Acoustic Consultant: Arup
Project Team: Jonathan Alotto, Jaenes Bong, Andrew Bromberg, Kevin Kasparek, Helena Lee, Thien Ly, David Prado, Jakub Riha, Hui Ee Wong

Dance and Music Centre, page 252
Client: ZRi adviseurs ingenieurs b.v.
Structural Engineer: Buro Happold
M&E Consultant: Buro Happold
Theatre and Acoustic Consultant: Artec Consultants Inc.
Landscape Consultant: Adrian L. Norman Ltd
Quantity Surveyor: Venue
Project Team: Andrew Bromberg, Billy Chan, Darren Chan, Henry Chan, Pong Chan, Pauline Gidoin, Ka-Ming Ho, Kevin Kasparek, Eugene Kiang, Willie Kau, Helena Lee, Francesco Lietti, Bonnie Liu, Vicky Pang, Maciej Setniewski, Tony Sin, Danny Tang, Jason Tang, Jason Yue

The Zheng He Cultural District, page 260
Client: Yanlord Land Group
Project Team: Jonathan Alotto, Andrew Bromberg, Kevin Chan, Te He, Kevin Kasparek, Janis Law, Helena Lee, Patti Lee, Huko Ma, Vienne Ma, Jakub Riha, Yundi Zhang

Project (Re)Plant, page 268
Client: Confidential
Project Team: Tony Ang, Jaenes Bong, Andrew Bromberg, Henry Chan, Olivia Chan, William Chi, Wang Kwoon Eng, Kevin Kwok, Patti Lee, Jakub Riha, Richard Tsang, Ian Wigmore, Gordon Yuen

HQ Beer Garden, page 274
Client: Confidential
Structural Engineer: Buro Happold
M&E Consultant: Meinhardt
Architect: Andrew Bromberg
Project Team: Jaenes Bong, Andrew Bromberg, Henry Chan, William Chi, Cai Hongkui, Anthony Ko, Kevin Kwok, Lawson Lai, Helena Lee, Patti Lee, Thien Ly, David Prado, Tiffany Szeto, Richard Tsang, Gordon Yuen

Picture Credits

Unless otherwise noted all images are © Andrew Bromberg at Aedas

Courtesy of the *Architectural Review*: 145 (bottom)
Courtesy of *A+U*: 130–131, 133 (bottom), 136 (bottom), 137, 140 (bottom), 141
Nic Arnold: 208 (bottom), 209 (top)
Virgile Simon Bertrand: 134–135, 138, 139 (top)
Andrew Bromberg: 28, 30 (top), 31, 37 (right), 90 (top), 198 (bottom right), 199 (right), 200 (top), 212 (bottom right)
Toby Chow: 25
Kerun Ip: 85 (top), 99 (bottom), 148 (top), 149 (bottom), 156–157, 160 (bottom), 212 (top, bottom left), 213, 214, 216, 252–253, 257 (top, bottom), 259, 274–275
Katherine Luna: 192–193, 194
Gerry O'Leary: 88–89, 91, 201
Courtesy of MTR: 30 (bottom)
Marcus Oleniuk: 84 (bottom), 85 (bottom), 86, 87 (top, bottom), 92, 145 (top), 147 (top), 196–197, 206–207, 208 (right),
Xiangdong Wang: 188 (top, bottom), 189
Paul Warchol: 2, 26–27, 34 (top), 36 (top, bottom), 37 (left), 82–83, 96 (bottom), 97, 100–101, 129, 132 (top), 136 (top), 142–143, 144 (top left), 146 (top, bottom), 147 (bottom), 151 (top), 186–187, 190, 191 (top, bottom), 210–211

Renderings
AsymmetricA: 38-39, 40 (top), 41 (right), 42–43, 44 (bottom), 45, 46 (top, left), 47 (bottom), 48–49, 52–53, 54 (top left, bottom), 55 (top, middle right), 56–57, 58 (top), 59, 60 (bottom), 61 (bottom), 62 (top, bottom), 63, 64, 108–109, 112, 152–153, 154 (bottom), 155 (top), 158 (bottom), 159 (top, bottom), 160 (top), 161, 162–163, 164 (bottom), 167, 233, 238–239, 240 (top), 242 (bottom), 243, 260–261, 263 (top), 264 (bottom), 265 (bottom), 266–267 (bottom), 267 (top), 268–269, 276 (bottom), 277 (top), 278, 279 (top), 290
Labtop: 168, 234–235, 236 (bottom), 236–237 (top), 241 (top), 242 (top)
LMNB: 50 (top right, top left), 51 (top right, bottom), 165 (top right, bottom left), 166, 202–203, 205, 244–245, 248–249, 251 (top)
Luxigon: 32 (top), 34 (bottom), 98 (bottom), 99 (top)
Adrian L. Norman Limited: 144 (bottom), 150 (bottom), 255 (top)
Silkroad: 94–95
Vyonyx Visualization: 102–103, 105, 107 (bottom), 185

Acknowledgments

Andrew Bromberg would like to thank Aaron Betsky, Lucas Dietrich, Keith Griffiths, Fleur Jones, Kevin Kasparek, Kam Kwan and the designers at Praline for their assistance in making this book.